SCHOLASTIC

Success With

Reading Tests

New York • Toronto • London • Auckland • Sydney
Mexico City • New Delhi • Hong Kong • Buenos Aires

Teaching
Resources

The *Scholastic Success With Reading Tests* series is designed to help you help students succeed on standardized tests. In this workbook for sixth grade, the 15 four-page tests are culled from the reading skills practice tests from *Scholastic News*, with some new and revised material. By familiarizing children with the skills, language, and formats they will encounter on state and national tests, these practice tests will boost confidence and help raise scores.

The questions supporting each test are specifically designed to review the following skills:

- Finding the Main Idea
- Reading for Detail
- Understanding Vocabulary
- Making Inferences
- Sequencing
- Understanding Cause and Effect
- Understanding Author's Purpose
- Understanding Fact and Opinion

Note that the tests in the second half of the book are slightly more difficult. These are designed to be given later in the school year.

In addition to helping children prepare for "real" tests, the practice tests in this workbook may be used as a diagnostic tool, to help you detect individual students' strengths and weaknesses, or as an instructional tool, for oral reading and discussion.

Keep in mind that our practice tests are just that—practice. These tests are not standardized. They should not be used to determine grade level, to compare one student's performance with that of others, or to evaluate teachers' abilities.

HOW TO ADMINISTER THE TESTS:

Before administering each test, you may wish to review with students some basic test-taking strategies, such as reading the questions before reading the passages.

- Establish a relaxed atmosphere. Explain to students that they will not be graded and that they are taking the test to practice for "real" tests down the road.
- Review the directions, then read the samples in each section and discuss the answers. Be sure to pay close attention to the directions in the vocabulary or study skills section on the last page of each test.
- To mimic the atmosphere of a real test, you may wish to set time limits. Students should be able to complete the reading comprehension section (the first three pages of each test) in 20 to 25 minutes. Allow an additional 10 minutes for the vocabulary or study skills portion on the last page of each test.
- Use the **Answer Key** provided on pages 63–64 to check students' work; or if desired, have students check their own answers.

> ## State Standards Correlations
>
> To find out how this book helps you meet your state's standards, log on to **www.scholastic.com/ssw**

Cover design by Ka-Yeon Kim-Li

ISBN 978-0-545-20108-7

24 25 26   40   21 20

Reading Skills Practice Test I

READING COMPREHENSION

Read each story. Then fill in the circle that best completes each sentence or answers each question.

SAMPLE

Despite their danger to humans, rattlesnakes rarely kill each other. When two rattlers fight, they never deliver a deadly bite. Instead, they lift their heads and push each other. The snake that gets pushed to the ground slinks away. The instinct not to kill each other helps keep the species alive.

I. What is the best title for this story?
○ **A.** "Endangered Snakes"
○ **B.** "Snakes of the World"
○ **C.** "How Rattlesnakes Fight"
○ **D.** "Rattlesnake Bites"

2. After a fight, a losing rattlesnake
○ **A.** bites the winner.
○ **B.** slinks away.
○ **C.** lifts its head.
○ **D.** dies.

A. The Maya were an ancient Central American people who developed a writing system. To write, they used picture symbols called hieroglyphs. They drew or carved the hieroglyphs on pottery, walls, and stone sculptures. Scholars who have learned to decipher Mayan hieroglyphs believe priests and nobles were the only people who could read this writing.

I. Hieroglyphs are
○ **A.** picture symbols.
○ **B.** ornaments.
○ **C.** pottery.
○ **D.** letters.

2. You can guess from the story that
○ **A.** the Maya were smarter than other people.
○ **B.** some Mayan hieroglyphs have been discovered.
○ **C.** hieroglyphs are a lot like our own form of writing.
○ **D.** hieroglyphs are colorful.

B. Do you know how to make rice? First, measure out the exact amount of rice you need. Then rinse the rice several times in cold water. Put it in a pot with exactly twice as much water as rice. Place the pot over medium heat and bring it to a boil. When it comes to a boil cover the pot tightly with a lid and turn the heat down very low. Let it cook for exactly 17 minutes. Don't peek! Then turn off the heat and let the pot of rice stand for another 5 minutes. Finally, fluff it with a fork.

1. What is the best title for this story?
   ○ **A.** "How to Cook Rice"
   ○ **B.** "Using the Stove"
   ○ **C.** "How to Serve Rice"
   ○ **D.** "Slow Cooking"

2. Right after you cover the pot with a lid, you should
   ○ **A.** rinse the rice.
   ○ **B.** turn down the heat.
   ○ **C.** add water.
   ○ **D.** fluff the rice with a fork.

3. The purpose of this story is to
   ○ **A.** inform.
   ○ **B.** persuade.
   ○ **C.** entertain.
   ○ **D.** inspire.

C. Scientists say houseplants do more than decorate homes and offices. They can also improve the quality of the air we breathe. Buildings today are often airtight and have plenty of insulation. This makes them energy-efficient, but it also makes it hard for fresh air to enter.

Many houseplants can "clean" the stale air trapped inside buildings. Plant leaves take in carbon dioxide gas from the air. In return, they give out clean oxygen. Plants also take other dangerous gases from the air. For instance, a type of daisy takes in benzene, a chemical found in gasoline. Spider plants take in carbon monoxide. So why not keep a lot of houseplants around? They just might help you breathe easier.

1. Spider plants take in
   ○ **A.** oxygen.
   ○ **B.** insulation.
   ○ **C.** benzene.
   ○ **D.** carbon monoxide.

2. Why can't fresh air enter many newer buildings?
   ○ **A.** They do not have enough spider plants.
   ○ **B.** They are airtight and have a lot of insulation.
   ○ **C.** They are too full of oxygen.
   ○ **D.** They have too many people.

3. Which of these is an *opinion* about plants?
   ○ **A.** They take in gas.
   ○ **B.** They look beautiful.
   ○ **C.** They give out oxygen.
   ○ **D.** They are found in some offices.

D.   Most parts of your body have a job to do. Not the appendix! The appendix is a three-inch-long, worm-shaped part of the intestines. While the appendix no longer appears to have a **function**, scientists think it was once an important part of the human digestive system. Some animals, like rabbits, still need an appendix. The organ helps them digest tough plant food.

Although the appendix may not do humans any good, it can do a lot of harm. If a person's appendix becomes infected by bacteria, he or she can suffer an attack of appendicitis. The symptoms include pain, nausea, and fever. If the appendix bursts, the infection can spread throughout the body. To prevent that from happening, a doctor will usually remove an infected appendix.

I.   The main idea of this story is that
- ○ **A.** humans and rabbits both have an appendix.
- ○ **B.** an appendix can burst.
- ○ **C.** the human appendix is not useful, but it is dangerous when infected.
- ○ **D.** every organ has a job.

2.   In this story the word **function** means
- ○ **A.** organ.
- ○ **B.** life.
- ○ **C.** job.
- ○ **D.** cause.

3.   You can guess from this story that
- ○ **A.** a person can live without an appendix.
- ○ **B.** a rabbit can live without an appendix.
- ○ **C.** the appendix is important.
- ○ **D.** humans never eat plants.

E.   Bolivia is a South American country that borders Peru, Chile, Argentina, Brazil, and Paraguay. It has a variety of landscapes. The north of Bolivia is mainly tropical rain forest. The Amazon River snakes through the steamy forest. Since there aren't many roads, people often travel through this area on riverboats. The forest is home to many kinds of wildlife, including toucans, jaguars, and capybaras, the world's largest rodents.

Bolivia's capital, La Paz, is in the snow-capped Andes mountains. At more than 12,000 feet, it is the highest capital in the world! Unlike the rainy, humid rain forest, this mountain area is extremely **arid**.

I.   In this story, the word **arid** means
- ○ **A.** wet.
- ○ **B.** hot.
- ○ **C.** dry.
- ○ **D.** cool.

2.   Bolivia's capital is special because
- ○ **A.** it's in the rain forest.
- ○ **B.** it's in the Andes.
- ○ **C.** it has capybaras.
- ○ **D.** it's the highest capital in the world.

3.   This story would probably go on to talk about
- ○ **A.** mountains.
- ○ **B.** other places in South America.
- ○ **C.** tropical birds.
- ○ **D.** North America.

VOCABULARY

Synonyms

Read the underlined word in each phrase. Mark the word below it that has the same (or close to the same) meaning.

Sample:

reluctant to go
- ○ **A.** eager
- ○ **C.** late
- ○ **B.** hesitant
- ○ **D.** surprised

1. gape at
   - ○ **A.** sneer
   - ○ **C.** smile
   - ○ **B.** squint
   - ○ **D.** stare

2. minor problems
   - ○ **A.** small
   - ○ **C.** difficult
   - ○ **B.** large
   - ○ **D.** easy

3. with liberty
   - ○ **A.** triumph
   - ○ **C.** freedom
   - ○ **B.** unwilling
   - ○ **D.** surprise

4. frail child
   - ○ **A.** unfriendly
   - ○ **C.** strong
   - ○ **B.** delicate
   - ○ **D.** feverish

5. perilous journey
   - ○ **A.** long
   - ○ **C.** interesting
   - ○ **B.** uncomfortable
   - ○ **D.** dangerous

6. squirming around
   - ○ **A.** standing
   - ○ **C.** laughing
   - ○ **B.** running
   - ○ **D.** wriggling

7. nonstop wailing
   - ○ **A.** crying
   - ○ **C.** talking
   - ○ **B.** speaking
   - ○ **D.** joking

Antonyms

Read the underlined word in each phrase. Mark the word below it that means the opposite or nearly the opposite.

Sample:

spectacular event
- ○ **A.** amazing
- ○ **C.** tragic
- ○ **B.** joyful
- ○ **D.** ordinary

1. driving recklessly
   - ○ **A.** cautiously
   - ○ **C.** slowly
   - ○ **B.** wildly
   - ○ **D.** carelessly

2. inferior brand
   - ○ **A.** exterior
   - ○ **C.** superior
   - ○ **B.** popular
   - ○ **D.** expensive

3. prolong the class
   - ○ **A.** lengthen
   - ○ **C.** join
   - ○ **B.** shorten
   - ○ **D.** begin

4. feel panic
   - ○ **A.** calm
   - ○ **C.** disgust
   - ○ **B.** upset
   - ○ **D.** content

5. amateur athlete
   - ○ **A.** gifted
   - ○ **C.** professional
   - ○ **B.** competitive
   - ○ **D.** untalented

6. unfortunate event
   - ○ **A.** important
   - ○ **C.** late
   - ○ **B.** early
   - ○ **D.** lucky

7. unfamiliar faces
   - ○ **A.** pleasant
   - ○ **C.** beautiful
   - ○ **B.** known
   - ○ **D.** strange

Reading Skills Practice Test 2

READING COMPREHENSION

Read each story. Then fill in the circle that best completes each sentence or answers each question.

Since 1870, the National Weather Service has been trying to do a very difficult job—predict the weather. Today, this government agency gives out a weather **forecast** four times a day. To make its forecasts, the Weather Service uses information collected from land stations, ships, and weather radars.

I. In this article the word **forecast** means
- ○ **A.** warning.
- ○ **B.** prediction.
- ○ **C.** sample.
- ○ **D.** hurricane.

2. What is the best title for this story?
- ○ **A.** "Weather Forecasting in 1870"
- ○ **B.** "You Can't Predict the Weather"
- ○ **C.** "The National Weather Service"
- ○ **D.** "Land Stations, Ships, and Weather Radars"

A. Peer **mediation** helps cut down on playground fighting and school suspensions. With peer mediation, kids in grades 4 to 12 are trained to settle arguments before they turn into fights. When a disagreement breaks out, two mediators step in. They listen to both sides and ask students how they want to see the problem resolved. If both kids agree to the terms, the mediators draw up a contract for each to sign. As long as they stick to the agreement, everyone wins!

Peer-mediation programs also boost the mediators' self-esteem. As one mediator said, "I learned I could help people."

I. In this story the word **mediation** means
- ○ **A.** resolving conflicts.
- ○ **B.** writing contracts.
- ○ **C.** using violence to end arguments.
- ○ **D.** ignoring conflicts.

2. This story is mostly about
- ○ **A.** playground fights.
- ○ **B.** new playground games.
- ○ **C.** ways to boost your self-esteem.
- ○ **D.** peer-mediation programs.

3. What do peer mediators do first?
- ○ **A.** They draw up a contract.
- ○ **B.** They listen to each side.
- ○ **C.** They ask a teacher for help.
- ○ **D.** They force both kids to agree.

B.   When people think about the countries of Europe, Andorra rarely comes to mind. That's probably because it's so tiny—just 180 square miles in all. It's located on the border of Spain and France, in a mountain range called the Pyrenees.

Andorra became independent in 1993. That year, its 50,000 citizens voted in elections for the very first time. Most Andorrans speak a language called Catalan. Like French and Spanish, Catalan is a Latin-based language.

Visitors come to Andorra to hike or ski in the mountains, and also to shop. Andorra has a low sales tax, so bargain hunters stream in from the neighboring countries. And there's no need to change currency; Andorra uses the Euro.

1. What is the best title for this story?
   ○ **A.** "The World's Tiniest Countries"
   ○ **B.** "Andorra, a Mountain Country"
   ○ **C.** "The Border of France and Spain"
   ○ **D.** "Why You Should Shop in Andorra"

2. From this article, you might guess that
   ○ **A.** France and Spain also have a low sales tax.
   ○ **B.** countries should charge sales tax.
   ○ **C.** Andorra will soon raise its sales tax.
   ○ **D.** both France and Spain probably have a higher sales tax.

3. Most Andorrans speak
   ○ **A.** Catalan.
   ○ **B.** Latin.
   ○ **C.** French.
   ○ **D.** Andorran.

C.   The world's tigers are roaring back to life. Tiger experts had once predicted the big cats would be nearly **extinct** by the year 2000. But in a recent report from the National Tiger Conservation Authority, conservationists, or people who save wildlife, agreed that the population of the largest member of the cat family appears to be on the rise.

Most tigers live in Asian nations, including Sumatra, Burma, India, and Thailand. In these countries, tigers have faced serious threats to their survival. Poachers, or people who kill wild animals and sell the body parts, hunted tigers for profit. Historically, many people in China have used tiger bones to make medicine for muscular aches and pains.

Now, many Asian countries are arresting poachers. And many Chinese people are trying to use alternatives to tiger bones for their medicines.

In the early 1970s, 50,000 to 70,000 tigers lived in Asia. Today, only a few thousand survive in the wild. But instead of falling even lower, the number is on the rise once again. In India, for example, the numbers have increased nearly 60% since 2008.

Now that's something to roar about!

1. Which is a *fact*?
   ○ **A.** Tigers belong in the zoo.
   ○ **B.** Most tigers live in Asian nations.
   ○ **C.** Most tigers are scary.
   ○ **D.** It's important to help save tigers.

2. How is the number of tigers in Asia today different from the number of tigers there in the 1970s?
   ○ **A.** There are fewer tigers in Asia today.
   ○ **B.** There are more tigers in Asia today.
   ○ **C.** There are the same number of tigers in Asia today.
   ○ **D.** There are no tigers in Asia today.

3. In this article, the word **extinct** means
   ○ **A.** smelly
   ○ **B.** alive
   ○ **C.** rising
   ○ **D.** dead

D. "I want to start a garden," Pablo told Mr. Cordiz, the store owner.

"Very good," Mr. Cordiz replied. "Which kinds of plants do you want to grow? They should be suited to the growing conditions in your backyard. Do you get a lot of sun?"

Pablo nodded his head yes.

Mr. Cordiz pointed to some plants with colorful blooms. "Snapdragons, poppies, and pansies are annuals," he said. "They start and finish their life cycles in one growing season. They will die in late fall. Sometimes they reseed themselves, but most likely next spring, you'll have to buy more and plant them again. These annuals like the sun."

Then, he pointed to some other plants in small plastic containers. "These are perennials. They will come back every year if you care for them properly. These hostas are perennials that grow very well in the shade. These peonies are sun-loving perennials. Their flowers are nice."

"I'll start with some perennials, please. I don't see the point of growing something that may not return next year," said Pablo.

I. Unlike perennials, annuals
○ **A.** must be grown in hanging baskets.
○ **B.** cannot be grown in the sun.
○ **C.** need plenty of shade.
○ **D.** finish their life cycles in a year.

2. You can conclude from this story that Pablo might have purchased
○ **A.** snapdragons.
○ **B.** pansies.
○ **C.** peonies.
○ **D.** poppies.

3. Which is an *opinion*?
○ **A.** Hostas grow well in the shade.
○ **B.** Hostas are a perennial.
○ **C.** Peonies grow well with lots of sun.
○ **D.** Peony flowers are nice.

E. Large numbers of Asian eels are eating up the small fish in ponds near Atlanta, Georgia. Without this important food source, the ponds' bigger fish may starve to death. To make matters worse, this eel problem is spreading to other areas.

The Asian eel is native to Southeast Asia and Australia. So how did these invaders get into U.S. ponds? Scientist John Biagi believes pet owners put them there. Baby Asian eels look like colorful little ribbons. As adults, however, they grow to three-feet long. Biagi says fish-tank owners who didn't realize they were raising such monsters set the adult eels free.

It may sound kind, but releasing the eels into the wild was the wrong thing to do, says Biagi. "The eels upset the ecosystem and may cause some native species to die out in the ponds."

I. Why may bigger fish starve to death?
○ **A.** Asian eels are eating all their food.
○ **B.** Large fish don't make good pets.
○ **C.** Big fish don't like Asian eels.
○ **D.** They have outgrown their ponds.

2. Which is an *opinion* about Asian eels?
○ **A.** They are eating up small fish.
○ **B.** They are native to Southeast Asia and Australia.
○ **C.** They can grow to three-feet long.
○ **D.** They are beautiful as babies.

3. This story would probably go on to talk about
○ **A.** which fish make the best pets.
○ **B.** fish people in Asia like to eat.
○ **C.** what to feed a pet Asian eel.
○ **D.** why releasing any kind of pet into the wild is not a good idea.

VOCABULARY

Synonyms

Read the underlined word in each phrase.
Mark the word below it that has the same
(or close to the same) meaning.

Sample:

essential equipment
- ○ **A.** necessary
- ○ **C.** cheap
- ○ **B.** expensive
- ○ **D.** sturdy

1. rigid material
   - ○ **A.** stiff
   - ○ **C.** natural
   - ○ **B.** red
   - ○ **D.** soft

2. elevate the book
   - ○ **A.** read
   - ○ **C.** describe
   - ○ **B.** criticize
   - ○ **D.** raise

3. became hysterical
   - ○ **A.** emotional
   - ○ **C.** tired
   - ○ **B.** calm
   - ○ **D.** energetic

4. a vague idea
   - ○ **A.** bad
   - ○ **C.** new
   - ○ **B.** sketchy
   - ○ **D.** great

5. an outlandish outfit
   - ○ **A.** outgrown
   - ○ **C.** silly
   - ○ **B.** handsome
   - ○ **D.** common

6. surprising triumph
   - ○ **A.** solution
   - ○ **C.** friend
   - ○ **B.** victory
   - ○ **D.** day

7. tattered clothing
   - ○ **A.** colorful
   - ○ **C.** worn-out
   - ○ **B.** new
   - ○ **D.** clean

Antonyms

Read the underlined word in each phrase.
Mark the word below it that means the
opposite or nearly the opposite.

Sample:

an efficient worker
- ○ **A.** busy
- ○ **C.** wasteful
- ○ **B.** hard
- ○ **D.** quick

1. a defiant attitude
   - ○ **A.** unhappy
   - ○ **C.** confused
   - ○ **B.** respectful
   - ○ **D.** poor

2. an earned privilege
   - ○ **A.** punishment
   - ○ **C.** treat
   - ○ **B.** paycheck
   - ○ **D.** position

3. the courage to persist
   - ○ **A.** speak
   - ○ **C.** act
   - ○ **B.** continue
   - ○ **D.** quit

4. renew the friendship
   - ○ **A.** end
   - ○ **C.** enjoy
   - ○ **B.** begin
   - ○ **D.** abuse

5. decline the offer
   - ○ **A.** ignore
   - ○ **C.** debate
   - ○ **B.** accept
   - ○ **D.** consider

6. valuable idea
   - ○ **A.** useful
   - ○ **C.** worthless
   - ○ **B.** super
   - ○ **D.** certain

7. nervous feeling
   - ○ **A.** calm
   - ○ **C.** angry
   - ○ **B.** frightened
   - ○ **D.** funny

Reading Skills Practice Test 3

READING COMPREHENSION

Read each story. Then fill in the circle that best completes each sentence or answers each question.

SAMPLE

There's no doubt about it. The world's most popular sport isn't basketball or baseball. It's soccer. Soccer is watched and played by far more people. Soccer's **astounding** popularity is shown by the size of the television audience for the World Cup. The World Cup is soccer's championship. Almost 1.5 billion people watched the 1998 World Cup final. The number grew to 3.2 billion in 2010, and even more in 2014!

I. In this passage the word **astounding** means
○ **A.** lack of.
○ **B.** amazing.
○ **C.** disappearing.
○ **D.** different.

2. What is the best title for this story?
○ **A.** "Soccer—The World's Favorite Sport"
○ **B.** "Soccer in America"
○ **C.** "Popular Television Programs"
○ **D.** "Baseball and Soccer Are My Favorite Games"

A. Have you ever heard a haiku? A haiku is a type of short poem that developed in Japan. Each haiku has only three lines and 17 syllables. The first and last lines have five syllables each. The second line has seven syllables.

Because of their small size, a haiku doesn't express long, complicated ideas. Usually, it simply tries to capture a single moment in time. Still, haiku is a very powerful form of poetry. Often, the subject is nature.

Although haiku developed years ago, the form is still popular in modern Japan. Many people make a hobby of composing haiku. Haiku clubs and magazines are also very popular.

I. How many syllables does a haiku contain?
○ **A.** 5
○ **B.** 7
○ **C.** 15
○ **D.** 17

2. You can conclude from this story that
○ **A.** Haikus are not as popular as they were in the past.
○ **B.** Every haiku contains images from nature.
○ **C.** Long poems are more interesting.
○ **D.** Haiku was developed in Japan.

B. The Tyrannosaurus rex (T. rex) roamed North America about 65 million years ago. For years, it was thought of as the king of meat-eating dinosaurs. It was a truly massive animal. It grew to 40 feet in length and weighed as much as seven tons. Recently, however, a new dino has been discovered. Its name is Giganotosaurus. It may be the real "king" dinosaur.

The discovery occurred in Argentina. Scientists found the fossils of the new dinosaur in the southern part of the country. Judging by its skeleton, the Giganotosaurus appears to outweigh the T. rex by as many as three tons. It may have been over 45 feet in length. The Giganotosaurus is also an older dinosaur. It lived about 100 million years ago.

1. The purpose of this article is to
○ **A.** amuse.   ○ **C.** persuade.
○ **B.** inform.   ○ **D.** sell a product.

2. What happened most recently?
○ **A.** The Giganotosaurus roamed the earth.
○ **B.** The Giganotosaurus was discovered.
○ **C.** The Tyrannosaurus roamed the earth.
○ **D.** The Tyrannosaurus was discovered.

3. You can conclude from this article that
○ **A.** scientists will never discover a bigger dinosaur than the Giganotosaurus.
○ **B.** scientists have learned everything there is to know about the Giganotosaurus.
○ **C.** scientists are still learning important things about dinosaurs.
○ **D.** T-rex and the Giganotosaurus were about the same weight.

C. No one had tried to break the window. It was simply an accident. Rosemary and Leslie were playing basketball in front of Rosemary's garage. As usual, Leslie had won.

It wasn't that Rosemary wasn't a skilled basketball player. In fact, she was exceptionally talented. She had a superior jump shot. She could dribble equally well with both hands. She was accomplished at grabbing rebounds. The trouble was that she easily became distracted. In the middle of a game she would see a neighbor's automobile drive by. Instead of **concentrating** on playing basketball, she would wave to say hello. Sometimes, in the middle of taking a shot, she would begin thinking about what she wanted for dinner.

Anyway, after the game was finished, Leslie threw the ball to Rosemary. As usual, however, Rosemary was thinking about something else. The ball sailed straight past her and through the living-room window.

"Oh no!" shouted Leslie. "We have to go and explain to your parents."

"You're right," said Rosemary. "Let's find them before they come to us."

1. In this story, the word **concentrating** means
○ **A.** hesitating.
○ **B.** forgetting about.
○ **C.** focusing on.
○ **D.** counting on.

2. According to the story, why does Leslie usually win games with Rosemary?
○ **A.** Rosemary always gets distracted.
○ **B.** Rosemary isn't very talented.
○ **C.** Rosemary is very talented.
○ **D.** Leslie is extremely talented.

3. How does Leslie seem to feel about the accident?
○ **A.** thrilled.   ○ **C.** happy.
○ **B.** upset.   ○ **D.** bored.

4. The next paragraph is likely to be about
○ **A.** Rosemary's new neighbor.
○ **B.** Leslie's favorite activities.
○ **C.** how Leslie learned to play basketball.
○ **D.** how Rosemary's parents react to the accident.

D. The Galápagos Islands are a special place. Located 600 miles from Ecuador's coast, they have all kinds of wildlife. About 5,000 species of plants and animals call the islands home. Many are unique. Animals like the Galápagos tortoise exist nowhere else in the world.

Sadly, some of these species are in danger. For example, the tortoise population has shrunk from 250,000 to less than 15,000. The number of sea lions has shrunk, too. So has the number of birds.

There are many different reasons why this wildlife is threatened. One reason is tourism. Since the 1960s, people have flocked to the islands. They come to see tortoises, iguanas, and penguins.

Today, about 65,000 tourists arrive every year. The crowds put stress on the fragile habitat. Their boats bring insects and other pests. These pests can harm the islands' native species.

I. The main idea of this article is that
○ **A.** the unique wildlife of the Galápagos is endangered.
○ **B.** insects can harm the islands' native species.
○ **C.** the Galápagos are located off Ecuador's coast.
○ **D.** one reason is tourism.

2. Which of these is an *opinion*?
○ **A.** There are 15,000 tortoises.
○ **B.** There were 250,000 tortoises.
○ **C.** The number of sea lions has shrunk.
○ **D.** The Galápagos are special.

3. You can infer from this story that
○ **A.** wildlife is the main attraction for visitors to the Galápagos.
○ **B.** the tortoise population will soon grow larger.
○ **C.** it used to be easier to get to the islands.
○ **D.** the tortoises rarely eat birds.

E. Have you ever thought about taking a long bike trip? These trips can be a lot of fun. Keep in mind, however, that you'll need to bring along the proper equipment. Carrying the essentials can mean the difference between a great trip and a bad one.

The most important piece of equipment is a helmet, naturally. A helmet will help to keep you safe if an accident occurs. A good helmet should fit snugly onto your head. A helmet that fits improperly might not provide you with sufficient protection. Other important items are a spare inner tube, a compact pump, and a multitool set. If you're in a distant place when a tire goes flat or a spoke comes loose, you'll be happy to have brought them along.

I. A helmet that doesn't fit properly
○ **A.** will usually protect the rider.
○ **B.** won't be as comfortable for the rider.
○ **C.** might not provide protection in an accident.
○ **D.** is an important piece of equipment.

2. The purpose of this article is to
○ **A.** make you laugh at how funny bike trips are.
○ **B.** inform you about what to bring on a bike trip.
○ **C.** persuade you not to go on bike trips.
○ **D.** tell you a story about a bike trip.

3. Which of the following is an *opinion*?
○ **A.** Long bike trips are fun.
○ **B.** A helmet can help keep you safe.
○ **C.** A helmet must fit properly to protect you.
○ **D.** A pump will be useful in case of a flat.

VOCABULARY

Synonyms

Read the underlined word in each phrase. Mark the word below it that has the same (or close to the same) meaning.

Sample:

sole survivor
- **A.** only
- **B.** lucky
- **C.** large
- **D.** silly

---

1. conceal the evidence
   - **A.** display
   - **B.** contribute
   - **C.** protect
   - **D.** hide

2. from another era
   - **A.** place
   - **B.** story
   - **C.** time period
   - **D.** community

3. beg to differ
   - **A.** gather
   - **B.** disagree
   - **C.** remain
   - **D.** be forgiven

4. cherish the moment
   - **A.** forget
   - **B.** detect
   - **C.** disgrace
   - **D.** treasure

5. hair-raising situation
   - **A.** terrifying
   - **B.** hilarious
   - **C.** awful
   - **D.** fast-moving

6. supreme confidence
   - **A.** absolute
   - **B.** little
   - **C.** surprising
   - **D.** inadequate

7. acquire knowledge
   - **A.** lose
   - **B.** gain
   - **C.** reject
   - **D.** reflect

Antonyms

Read the underlined word in each phrase. Mark the word below it that means the opposite or nearly the opposite.

Sample:

create chaos
- **A.** chatter
- **B.** noise
- **C.** disturbance
- **D.** order

---

1. a flimsy excuse
   - **A.** unbelievable
   - **B.** early
   - **C.** late
   - **D.** solid

2. oppose the motion
   - **A.** tighten
   - **B.** support
   - **C.** cease
   - **D.** oppress

3. considerable expense
   - **A.** costly
   - **B.** worthwhile
   - **C.** unfortunate
   - **D.** insignificant

4. appropriate action
   - **A.** fast
   - **B.** unsuitable
   - **C.** discouraging
   - **D.** brazen

5. vague idea
   - **A.** precise
   - **B.** vacant
   - **C.** unclear
   - **D.** uneven

6. betray the cause
   - **A.** disturb
   - **B.** believe
   - **C.** support
   - **D.** understand

7. reckless behavior
   - **A.** careless
   - **B.** careful
   - **C.** proud
   - **D.** humble

Reading Skills Practice Test 4

READING COMPREHENSION

Read each story. Then fill in the circle that best completes each sentence or answers each question.

Is red just red and green just green? Apparently not, say **authorities** on the subject of color. In every culture, colors have meanings. And each culture looks at specific colors in different ways.

White, for example, is a popular choice for American wedding gowns. In Japan, however, brides who prefer a traditional Shinto ceremony will not wear it. For them, white is associated with mourning and wearing it at a wedding is considered unlucky.

Blue is the most accepted color around the world, authorities say. Few cultures assign blue a negative meaning, perhaps because it is the color of water and sky.

I. In this passage, the word **authorities** means
- ○ **A.** witnesses.
- ○ **B.** experts.
- ○ **C.** countries.
- ○ **D.** animals.

2. What is the best title for this story?
- ○ **A.** "Water and Sky"
- ○ **B.** "Japanese Bridal Traditions"
- ○ **C.** "The Meaning of Blue"
- ○ **D.** "The Meaning of Colors"

A. For 15 centuries, people have argued about the Loch Ness monster. Is there really a monster living deep in the beautiful Scottish lake? Those who claim that "Nessie" exists point to strange disturbances in the water. Sometimes the surface ripples. It bubbles and shakes. Occasionally, a hump, like a dinosaur's, seems to appear.

Recently, an Italian scientist came up with a "non-monsterly" cause for these events. Luigi Piccardi points to the Great Glen Fault that runs under the lake. A fault is a fissure in the earth. Faults can cause gas eruptions, roaring sounds, and earthquakes. According to Piccardi, these kinds of things cause the disturbances, not a monster.

I. Luigi Piccardi maintains that
- ○ **A.** the Great Glen Fault explains "Nessie" sightings.
- ○ **B.** there are no disturbances in Loch Ness.
- ○ **C.** the Loch Ness monster exists.
- ○ **D.** the Loch Ness monster caused the Great Glen Fault.

2. Which of these is an *opinion*?
- ○ **A.** Faults can cause gas eruptions and earthquakes.
- ○ **B.** Disturbances have occurred in the surface of the lake.
- ○ **C.** The Great Glen Fault runs beneath Loch Ness.
- ○ **D.** The Loch Ness monster exists.

B.   Experiencing nature is great, but when backpacking, fishing, or hiking in the woods, always keep safety in mind. Remembering several important rules can keep a wilderness **excursion** from turning into tragedy.

First, be prepared for weather changes. Always pack warm clothes and rainwear, just in case! This is particularly true in the mountains. The weather at high altitude is notoriously fickle.

Second, carry a map, compass, and flashlight. Even experienced hikers get lost. You should be familiar with your route before you start your trip. Study the map to get to know the area and any landmarks on the way. The flashlight is important if you do get lost. Many trips that start out in daylight become nighttime adventures when people can't find their way.

Third, bring a first-aid kit and know how to use it. Small scrapes can be more serious when there is no doctor nearby. Finally, tell people where you are going and when you plan to come back. That way, someone will go look for you in case trouble strikes.

I. In this story, the word **excursion** means
  ○ **A.** truck.   ○ **C.** journey.
  ○ **B.** vehicle.   ○ **D.** discussion.

2. What is the best title for this story?
  ○ **A.** "First Aid in the Mountains"
  ○ **B.** "Don't Get Lost"
  ○ **C.** "Wilderness Safety Tips"
  ○ **D.** "The Danger of Nature"

3. The purpose of this article is to
  ○ **A.** amuse.   ○ **C.** inform.
  ○ **B.** frighten.   ○ **D.** sell a product.

C.   Should people be allowed to drive while talking on a cell phone? This question is being asked more and more frequently. New York became the first state in the nation to ban handheld cell-phone use while driving. Other cities, states, and municipalities have followed New York's lead.

Critics of cell phones say that talking on the phone while driving is a safety issue. They argue that cell-phone chatter is distracting. When people pay attention to the phone, they don't pay attention to the road. This can lead to accidents and even deaths. According to one study, people who gab on the phone while driving may be four times more likely to get into an accident. Many motorists have been cut off or nearly hit by drivers deep in chat.

Critics of the cell-phone ban argue that there is no *proof* that talking on the phone is more dangerous than other activities. Modern cars are filled with electronic distractions. Drivers can get into accidents while changing the station on their radios. Why not ban people from eating while they drive? Or from talking to passengers in the back seat?

I. What is illegal in New York?
  ○ **A.** using handheld cell phones
  ○ **B.** eating while driving
  ○ **C.** changing radio stations while
      driving
  ○ **D.** using handheld cell phones while
      driving

2. Critics of the cell-phone ban argue that
  ○ **A.** many different activities can distract
      drivers.
  ○ **B.** cell phones never distract drivers.
  ○ **C.** cell phones always distract drivers.
  ○ **D.** cell phones save lives.

3. You can infer from this story that
  ○ **A.** all drivers now use cell phones.
  ○ **B.** soon all drivers will use cell phones.
  ○ **C.** driving in a car may become more
      dangerous.
  ○ **D.** more states may enact laws about
      cell phones and driving.

D. "I could never possibly do it," I said. I meant it, seriously! My sister Pilar had been describing how much she loved scuba diving. We were spending two weeks at the beach, and she had just finished her initial underwater dive. She raved about the brightly colored coral, the anemones, the turtles, and even the shark that she had observed.

"It's like another world down there, James," said Pilar. "There's the world on dry land and the world beneath the water; the only way you can see that world is by putting on a scuba mask and oxygen tank. It's not actually dangerous. You get trained on the proper usage of the equipment, and the instructor is always present. If an emergency occurs, you're completely prepared."

"I don't care about another world," I replied, "I don't want to be eaten by sharks and what if I run out of oxygen? I'm a dry-land type of guy."

My sister is very **persistent**, however, and before the first week was up, I was enrolled in scuba instruction against my will. Pilar was waiting when I surfaced from my first dive. "Well?" she said. "Wow, Pilar. It is another world!" I shouted.

I. At first, how does James seem to feel about diving?
- ○ **A.** excited
- ○ **B.** terrified
- ○ **C.** bored
- ○ **D.** interested

2. How does James react to his first dive?
- ○ **A.** He seems to be thrilled.
- ○ **B.** He seems angry.
- ○ **C.** He seems disappointed.
- ○ **D.** He seems somewhat satisfied.

3. In this story, **persistent** means
- ○ **A.** determined.
- ○ **B.** prudent.
- ○ **C.** agitated.
- ○ **D.** calm.

E. Some people call it the "Roof of the World." The country is Bhutan. It's a tiny kingdom high in the mountains of the Himalayas. Bhutan shares its borders with China and India, the world's two most populous countries. But compared with those giants, Bhutan is microscopic. It's only about half the size of Indiana, and has fewer than one million inhabitants.

Bhutan gained independence in 1947. The country's name means "Land of the Thunder Dragon," a reference to the severe storms that roar through the Himalayas. These rugged mountains dominate the country. They also keep it isolated from the rest of the world. There are only two airlines that fly to Bhutan. Up until 1962, the country had no postal service or paved roads. Now, it is slowly modernizing. Television finally arrived in 1999. Bhutan was the first nation to ban smoking.

Not many people get the chance to visit this tiny country, but those who do get to see the Bhutanese way of life, the mountains, and the forests. Bhutan has a remarkable diversity of wildlife, hundreds of species of birds, and 5,000 plants. These attractions never fail to thrill the visitors.

I. Which of these is an *opinion*?
- ○ **A.** The country's name means "Land of the Thunder Dragon."
- ○ **B.** Bhutan's attractions never fail to thrill visitors.
- ○ **C.** Until 1962, the country had no postal service.
- ○ **D.** Bhutan has 5,000 species of plants.

2. Compared to India and China, Bhutan
- ○ **A.** has a far greater diversity of wildlife.
- ○ **B.** has many visitors.
- ○ **C.** is very modern.
- ○ **D.** is a very small country.

3. Which happened most recently?
- ○ **A.** Television arrived in Bhutan.
- ○ **B.** Bhutan's first paved road was built.
- ○ **C.** Bhutan became independent.
- ○ **D.** Bhutan developed a postal service.

VOCABULARY

Synonyms

Read the underlined word in each phrase. Mark the word below it that has the same (or close to the same) meaning.

Sample:

fabulous recipe
- A. excellent
- B. tasteless
- C. difficult
- D. frivolous

1. humiliating event
- A. successful
- B. embarrassing
- C. disturbing
- D. frightening

2. capable hands
- A. able
- B. unable
- C. clumsy
- D. fast

3. looking for insight
- A. contentment
- B. understanding
- C. courtesy
- D. forgiveness

4. supreme confidence
- A. absolute
- B. little
- C. surprising
- D. inadequate

5. acquire knowledge
- A. lose
- B. gain
- C. reject
- D. reflect

6. take a stroll
- A. look
- B. number
- C. board
- D. walk

7. waterfront location
- A. central
- B. mountainous
- C. island
- D. shore

Antonyms

Read the underlined word in each phrase. Mark the word below it that means the opposite or nearly the opposite.

Sample:

artificial flavoring
- A. superficial
- B. delicious
- C. unusual
- D. natural

1. overtake the leader
- A. overwhelm
- B. obstruct
- C. fall behind
- D. rejoin

2. considerable amount
- A. strange
- B. expensive
- C. small
- D. large

3. beg to differ
- A. digest
- B. defer
- C. agree
- D. assume

4. betray the cause
- A. disturb
- B. believe
- C. support
- D. understand

5. reckless behavior
- A. careless
- B. careful
- C. proud
- D. humble

6. tighten the hold
- A. return
- B. remove
- C. slow
- D. loosen

7. possible solution
- A. problem
- B. surprise
- C. activity
- D. idea

Reading Skills Practice Test 5

READING COMPREHENSION

Read each story. Then fill in the circle that best completes each sentence or answers each question.

SAMPLE

When an iguana's food supply shrinks, so does its bone structure. Iguanas living in Ecuador's Galapagos Islands increase their chances of survival by shrinking in length as much as 20 percent. When the food supply is **bountiful**, the iguanas grow back to their original size. Scientists hope further study of the iguanas will lead to finding new treatments for human bone diseases.

I. In this passage, the word **bountiful** means
- ○ **A.** plentiful
- ○ **B.** dangerous
- ○ **C.** disappearing
- ○ **D.** safe

2. What is the best title for this passage?
- ○ **A.** "Bone Diseases"
- ○ **B.** "Good Food Is Hard to Find"
- ○ **C.** "Iguanas Shrink to Survive"
- ○ **D.** "Ecuador"

A. Scientists recently found a 290-million-year-old fossil, or imprint in rock, which they say is proof that an early reptile ran faster than any other living creature at that time—and it did it on two legs! The reptile, less than one foot long, was running around on its two back legs 80 million years before the first known dinosaur did so. This means the newly **discovered** reptile named Eudibamus cursoris (you-da-bom-us cur-sor-us) is the first known creature to walk on its two back legs. The reptile likely ran in an upright position, like humans and some dinosaurs. Scientists believe the reptile started running upright so it could escape the hungry meat-eaters that hunted it.

I. What can you conclude is the most important aspect of this fossil discovery?
- ○ **A.** The fossil shows the first reptile that moved on its two back legs.
- ○ **B.** The fossil is an imprint of a reptile that is found in a rock.
- ○ **C.** The fossil is 290 million years old.
- ○ **D.** The reptile was less than one foot long.

2. In this story, the word **discovered** means
- ○ **A.** insulted.
- ○ **B.** closed.
- ○ **C.** found.
- ○ **D.** invented.

3. Scientists believe that the reptile started running upright on its two back legs because
- ○ **A.** it was sick of going around on four legs.
- ○ **B.** it was only one foot long, which was too short to walk on four legs.
- ○ **C.** it was trying to escape the hungry meat-eaters that hunted it.
- ○ **D.** it ran faster than all other creatures.

B. Eliza Yellow Bird sits in bleachers surrounded by fans yelling nasty comments at the Fighting Sioux hockey team of the University of North Dakota. The 12-year-old tries to ignore the shouts, but every insult feels like a punch in the stomach.

"They'll yell, 'The Sioux stink. The Sioux are losers,'" says Eliza, who is Native American. "It makes me feel angry because it's like they're saying it against the Sioux tribe and all Indians."

Eliza is among thousands of Native Americans and others who are speaking out against sports teams that use Indian logos, nicknames, and mascots. They say that these symbols—along with "Indian" war chants and halftime dances—mock, or make fun of, their culture. They say that images of Indians wearing face paint and feathers are stereotypes. A stereotype is an overly simple picture or opinion of a person, group, or thing.

"Stereotypes keep people from seeing who Native Americans are today," says Christine Munson, co-chair of the Youth Indian Mascot and Logo Task Force, an organization fighting to get rid of Indian mascots and logos from Wisconsin public schools. "We don't live in tepees. We don't always walk around with feathers in our hair. We're police officers, lawyers, professors, and business owners."

1. How did Eliza feel when she heard hockey fans yelling nasty comments at the Fighting Sioux hockey team?
○ **A.** angry
○ **B.** proud
○ **C.** tired
○ **D.** happy

2. From this article, you can conclude that
○ **A.** most Native Americans go to hockey games.
○ **B.** many Native Americans want teams to stop using Indian logos, nicknames and mascots.
○ **C.** Eliza Yellow Bird wants to be a lawyer when she grows up.
○ **D.** teams use Indian logos, nicknames and mascots out of respect for Native Americans.

3. Which would be the best title for this article?
○ **A.** "Fighting Stereotypes of Native Americans"
○ **B.** "The Sioux"
○ **C.** "The Trouble With Teams"
○ **D.** "Eliza Yellow Bird: Explaining Indian Names"

C. For people in China and other Chinese communities around the world, the New Year does not begin on January 1. Instead, it falls in January or February, and lasts for two weeks.

Chinese New Year traditions include exchanging gifts and decorating houses in red—a good luck color. Chinese families might also eat rice cakes for good luck, and dumplings for family togetherness.

"People all over the world celebrate Chinese New Year," says Nancy Jervis of the China Institute in New York. "It's not just for people in China."

Legend says that Buddha (boo-duh), a religious leader, invited the world's creatures to visit, and named each year on the Chinese calendar after the 12 animals that came. The year 2013 was the year of the snake, 2014 was the year of the horse, and 2015 was the year of the sheep.

1. Chinese New Year lasts for
○ **A.** 1 day.
○ **B.** 5 days.
○ **C.** 14 days.
○ **D.** 12 days.

2. At Chinese New Year, the color red represents
○ **A.** family togetherness.
○ **B.** Buddha.
○ **C.** China.
○ **D.** good luck.

3. The purpose of this article is to tell you about
○ **A.** Chinese New Year.
○ **B.** Chinese traditions.
○ **C.** the China Institute in New York.
○ **D.** the Buddha.

D. When Jordy Brown was five, his dad came home from a trip to Mexico with a poster from a bullfight. Jordy thought it looked cruel. He made his dad promise never to go to a bullfight again. But Jordy didn't stop there. The 11-year-old from Irvine, California, wanted to end bullfights for good. Jordy **launched** a letter-writing campaign and petition drive to convince Mexican leaders to stop bullfights. Jordy also adopted two baby bulls named Rocky and Ben. Jordy sends money to people who own the bulls to help care for them and keep them safe.

Jordy says anyone who looks into a bull's eyes knows it's a creature that deserves respect. "Bulls have beautiful eyes," Jordy says. "They are really sweet animals."

1. In this article, the word **launched** means
- ❍ **A.** sailed.
- ❍ **C.** ended.
- ❍ **B.** wrote.
- ❍ **D.** began.

2. Jordy first learned about bullfights
- ❍ **A.** on television.
- ❍ **B.** when he saw two bulls up for adoption.
- ❍ **C.** through a letter-writing campaign and petition drive.
- ❍ **D.** when his father came home from Mexico with a poster from a bullfight.

3. Which of these is a *fact*?
- ❍ **A.** Bullfighting is wrong.
- ❍ **B.** Bulls have beautiful eyes.
- ❍ **C.** Jordy adopted two baby bulls named Rocky and Ben.
- ❍ **D.** Jordy should adopt more baby bulls.

E. Greg Bossart's job takes him all over the globe, from Iraq to Brazil—and he doesn't even have to wear shoes. Instead, he suits up to go beneath the water, curing patients of disease or helping them out of dangerous situations. Dr. Bossart is an aquavet, an aquatic veterinarian specially trained to take care of animals with fins or flippers. Aquavets swim to the rescue when sea otters and other water creatures are not feeling well.

"I always wanted a job where I didn't have to wear shoes," says Dr. Bossart. "I feel most blessed to work with some of the most intellectually **stimulating** animals."

Fewer than 100 veterinarians in the U.S. are experienced in caring for underwater creatures. The importance of aquatic veterinarians was highlighted in 1989 when they were sent to clean and treat otters covered in oil after an Alaskan oil spill.

In 1991, Dr. Bossart was asked to help out when sea turtles and marine mammals were threatened by oil that was dumped in the gulf after the Persian Gulf War. Bossart taught others how to clean animals covered in oil with nontoxic dishwashing liquid.

1. Dr. Greg Bossart doesn't wear shoes while he works because
- ❍ **A.** he likes to wear sneakers.
- ❍ **B.** he works in the water.
- ❍ **C.** veterinarians never wear shoes.
- ❍ **D.** people in other countries don't wear shoes.

2. In this article, the word **stimulating** means
- ❍ **A.** exciting.
- ❍ **B.** harmful.
- ❍ **C.** intelligent.
- ❍ **D.** stinging.

3. What was similar about the emergencies of 1989 and 1991?
- ❍ **A.** No animals were hurt either time.
- ❍ **B.** Otters were harmed both times.
- ❍ **C.** Dr. Bossart worked with 100 other aquavets both times.
- ❍ **D.** In both situations, oil was spilled into the water.

VOCABULARY

Synonyms

Read the underlined word in each phrase. Mark the word below it that has the same (or nearly the same) meaning.

Sample:

loathe his enemy
- ○ **A.** hate
- ○ **B.** love
- ○ **C.** fix
- ○ **D.** leave

1. mimic her
   - ○ **A.** please
   - ○ **B.** show
   - ○ **C.** hurt
   - ○ **D.** imitate

2. distinct sound
   - ○ **A.** clear
   - ○ **B.** boring
   - ○ **C.** quiet
   - ○ **D.** unpleasant

3. inhale deeply
   - ○ **A.** sleep
   - ○ **B.** breathe out
   - ○ **C.** dig
   - ○ **D.** breathe in

4. remain still
   - ○ **A.** play
   - ○ **B.** sit
   - ○ **C.** stay
   - ○ **D.** lie

5. massive stadium
   - ○ **A.** filled
   - ○ **B.** small
   - ○ **C.** dark
   - ○ **D.** huge

6. serene expression
   - ○ **A.** peaceful
   - ○ **B.** uncertain
   - ○ **C.** shy
   - ○ **D.** happy

7. distinctive quality
   - ○ **A.** boring
   - ○ **B.** freakish
   - ○ **C.** normal
   - ○ **D.** unusual

Multiple Meanings

Read both sentences in each set. Then choose the one word that correctly completes both sentences.

Sample:

She went home to _____ her clothes before soccer practice.
His pockets were filled with loose _____.
- ○ **A.** wash
- ○ **B.** change
- ○ **C.** gather
- ○ **D.** find

1. Are you going to _____ that you took the cookie from the jar?
   This ticket will only _____ one person to the movie.
   - ○ **A.** bring
   - ○ **B.** admit
   - ○ **C.** say
   - ○ **D.** invite

2. The cat disappeared one day without a _____.
   He wants see-through paper so he can _____ the picture in the book.
   - ○ **A.** sound
   - ○ **B.** sign
   - ○ **C.** trace
   - ○ **D.** draw

3. We eat a turkey every Thanksgiving because it's our _____.
   She had her wedding dress _____ made to fit her perfectly.
   - ○ **A.** favorite
   - ○ **B.** custom
   - ○ **C.** dinner
   - ○ **D.** home

4. He read in the paper about the army's _____ towards enemy territory.
   I asked my mother if I could have an _____ on my allowance.
   - ○ **A.** movement
   - ○ **B** extra
   - ○ **C.** advance
   - ○ **D.** shot

Reading Skills Practice Test 6

READING COMPREHENSION

Read each story. Then fill in the circle that best completes each sentence or answers each question.

Do not expect to see the snowshoe rabbit after a snowfall. As the weather grows cold, the fur on this **creature** changes from brown to white. Then it cannot be seen against a snowy landscape.

I. What is the best title for this story?
- ○ **A.** "Brown Fur"
- ○ **B.** "Winter Snow"
- ○ **C.** "Snowshoe Rabbits"
- ○ **D.** "All About Rabbits"

2. In this story, the word **creature** means
- ○ **A.** monster.
- ○ **B.** animal.
- ○ **C.** foot.
- ○ **D.** clothing.

A. As a young girl, Sally Ride was fascinated by outer space. In college, she, studied science. When NASA, the National Aeronautics and Space Administration, was looking for new astronauts to train, Ride applied. She was one of only 35 accepted. This was the first time NASA allowed women into the training program.

During training, Ride learned how to move around in space, **operate** machines in a spacecraft, and fly a jet. On June 18, 1983, she blasted off of the space shuttle Challenger. She became America's first female astronaut.

I. This story is mainly about
- ○ **A.** NASA.
- ○ **B.** space.
- ○ **C.** Sally Ride.
- ○ **D.** women.

2. In this story, the word **operate** means
- ○ **A.** use.
- ○ **B.** clean.
- ○ **C.** take apart.
- ○ **D.** cut open.

3. This story would probably go on to talk about
- ○ **A.** Ride's childhood.
- ○ **B.** why Ride likes science.
- ○ **C.** the planets.
- ○ **D.** what Ride did as an astronaut.

B. Your funny bone is not a bone at all! It is really a nerve—the ulnar nerve. It runs from your shoulders to your fingers. Its job is to send messages from your arm to your brain. The ulnar nerve is near one of your arm bones, the humerus. Humerus sounds like *humorous*, which means funny. But everyone knows that when you hit your funny bone, it's nothing to laugh about!

I. What is the best title for this story?
- ○ **A.** "Your Skeleton"
- ○ **B.** "Humorous Jokes"
- ○ **C.** "The Funny Bone"
- ○ **D.** "What Makes You Laugh?"

2. You can guess that
- ○ **A.** nerves look like bones.
- ○ **B.** hitting the ulnar nerve hurts.
- ○ **C.** the funny bone tickles.
- ○ **D.** few people have an ulnar nerve.

C. The giant Rocky Mountain chain stretches all the way from New Mexico to Alaska. Today, the Rockies are a popular spot for mining, hiking, and skiing. But in the early 1800s, the Rockies were just in the way! When settlers headed west, they had a hard time crossing these steep cliffs. Finally, in the 1840s, pioneers cut a route through the Rockies called the Oregon Trail.

I. The Rockies were in the way of
- ○ **A.** hikers.
- ○ **B.** settlers.
- ○ **C.** miners.
- ○ **D.** skiers.

2. The author wrote this story to
- ○ **A.** convince people to ski.
- ○ **B.** tell the history of Oregon.
- ○ **C.** tell the history of the Rockies.
- ○ **D.** tell how mountains form.

D. During winter, some people feel unhappy and have trouble concentrating.

Doctors call these winter **blues** SAD, or Seasonal Affective Disorder. Scientists believe people get SAD because there is less daylight in winter than in other seasons.

This lack of light can affect the body. To help people with SAD, doctors find ways for them to get more light. For example, patients might sit in front of a light box or spend more time outside.

I. The main idea of this story is
- ○ **A.** winter is dangerous.
- ○ **B.** less light makes some people feel sad.
- ○ **C.** people need to exercise.
- ○ **D.** all seasons are the same.

2. In this story, the word **blues** means
- ○ **A.** sadness.
- ○ **B.** colors.
- ○ **C.** music.
- ○ **D.** winter.

3. Going outside helps people with SAD because
- ○ **A.** fresh air is good.
- ○ **B.** they need less light.
- ○ **C.** they need exercise.
- ○ **D.** they need more light.

E.   California condors are the largest birds in North America. But these flying giants are in danger of dying out. Experts are trying to save condors by catching them and raising their young in a safe environment. When they are old enough, the condor chicks are released.

Scientists fear these condor chicks may not know enough about the dangers of life on their own. Some have flown into power lines—the wires and cables that carry electricity. Many young condors have gotten hurt or killed. Now, people in places where condors live want to bury power lines to keep condors safe.

1. What happens to some condors after they are released?
  ○ **A.** They fly to California.
  ○ **B.** They are raised by experts.
  ○ **C.** They hurt other animals.
  ○ **D.** They are hurt or killed.

2. You can guess that
  ○ **A.** people care about condors.
  ○ **B.** condors will soon die out.
  ○ **C.** power lines are too long.
  ○ **D.** there are too many condors.

3. Which of these is an *opinion* about condors?
  ○ **A.** They are birds.
  ○ **B.** They are in danger.
  ○ **C.** They live in the U.S.
  ○ **D.** They are ugly.

F.   There are two types of garbage. Natural garbage such as an apple core is biodegradable. It will rot over time. Manufactured garbage, such as a plastic bag, is not biodegradable. It will stay the same for hundreds of years. Luckily, much of our manufactured garbage can be recycled. This will **prevent** our planet from filling up with trash. To find out if your trash is biodegradable, try this test:
  1. Fill several flower pots with damp soil.
  2. Find some small pieces of garbage.
  3. Bury one piece of garbage in each flower pot.
  4. Write labels to show what is buried in each flower pot.
  5. Place the pots in a cool, damp place.
  6. After a few weeks, dig up the buried pieces of garbage. Which pieces didn't rot? Check to see if your community recycles this type of trash.

1. In this story, the word **prevent** means
  ○ **A.** stop.
  ○ **B.** grow.
  ○ **C.** help.
  ○ **D.** build.

2. What should you do right after you put the pots in a cool place?
  ○ **A.** Bury pieces of trash.
  ○ **B.** Wait a few weeks.
  ○ **C.** Find some flower pots.
  ○ **D.** Dig up the garbage.

3. You would probably find this story in a book about
  ○ **A.** flower pots.
  ○ **B.** recycling.
  ○ **C.** dirt.
  ○ **D.** aluminum.

4. You can guess that
  ○ **A.** recycling is a waste of time.
  ○ **B.** trash is dangerous.
  ○ **C.** dirt helps some garbage rot.
  ○ **D.** we should bury all trash.

STUDY SKILLS
Reading a Line Graph

Study this line graph about immigration to the U.S. Then choose the best answer for each question.

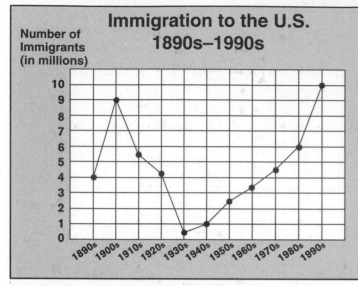

Immigration to the U.S. 1890s–1990s

1. This line graph shows immigration
   - ○ **A.** before 1870.
   - ○ **B.** to Europe.
   - ○ **C.** from the 1890s to 1990s.
   - ○ **D.** from Europe and Asia only.

2. The fewest immigrants arrived in the
   - ○ **A.** 1930s.
   - ○ **C.** 1940s.
   - ○ **B.** 1900s.
   - ○ **D.** 1950s.

3. About how many immigrants arrived in the U.S. in the 1980s?
   - ○ **A.** 6 thousand
   - ○ **C.** 5.5 million
   - ○ **B.** 6 million
   - ○ **D.** 4.5 million

4. What can you tell about the 1920s?
   - ○ **A.** There were fewer than 3 million immigrants.
   - ○ **B.** Immigration reached its peak.
   - ○ **C.** Most immigrants were Asian.
   - ○ **D.** There were just over 4 million immigrants.

Reading a Table of Contents

A table of contents shows what you will find in a book. This table is from a book called *Life in the Sea*.

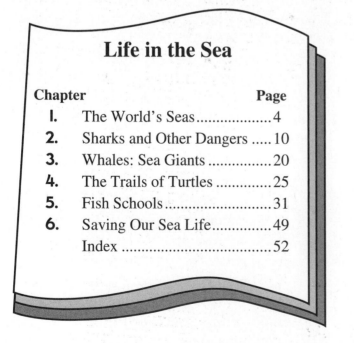

Life in the Sea

1. If you want to know about how turtles travel, read chapter
   - ○ **A.** three.
   - ○ **C.** five.
   - ○ **B.** four.
   - ○ **D.** six.

2. The longest chapter in the book is chapter
   - ○ **A.** three.
   - ○ **C.** five.
   - ○ **B.** four.
   - ○ **D.** six.

3. You can guess that chapter six will talk about
   - ○ **A.** the best places for fishing.
   - ○ **B.** protecting sea animals.
   - ○ **C.** moving sea animals to new homes.
   - ○ **D.** how fish form schools.

4. Which animal will you probably not find in this book?
   - ○ **A.** octopus
   - ○ **C.** seal
   - ○ **B.** blue whale
   - ○ **D.** panda

Reading Skills Practice Test 7

READING COMPREHENSION

Read each story. Then fill in the circle that best completes each sentence or answers each question.

SAMPLE

Fifty years ago, thousands of wild Siberian tigers roamed freely across a large part of Asia—in Siberia, China, and North and South Korea. Today, only about 400 of these great cats survive. Unless **drastic** measures are taken, the tiger may be extinct in the near future.

1. In this passage, the word **drastic** means
○ **A.** serious.
○ **B.** natural.
○ **C.** small.
○ **D.** many.

2. What is the best title for this story?
○ **A.** "The Countries of Asia"
○ **B.** "Endangered Animals"
○ **C.** "Tigers Born in Zoos"
○ **D.** "The Siberian Tiger"

A. One day in 1619, a tradesman working for the Virginia Company in Jamestown, Virginia, purchased goods from a Dutch warship anchored in the harbor. The tradesman was just doing his job—buying, selling, and trading goods. But there was one large difference about the job he did that day. The "goods" he purchased were human beings. He bought 20 captive Africans from that Dutch ship. It was the first time in recorded history that African slaves were sold in America.

After that, the slave business boomed, and many more ships arrived. By 1860, the U.S. had about 4 million slaves. They were Africans who had been snatched from their homeland and sold into bondage, along with thousands of their descendants who were born on American soil.

1. The first slaves were sold in America
○ **A.** in 1619.
○ **B.** in 1916.
○ **C.** in 1860.
○ **D.** in 1680.

2. The next paragraph is likely to be about
○ **A.** Dutch warships.
○ **B.** slavery in the United States.
○ **C.** the Virginia Company.
○ **D.** African kingdoms.

3. You can conclude from this story that
○ **A.** all enslaved Africans arrived the same year.
○ **B.** slavery was not profitable in the colonies.
○ **C.** all American slaves came from those first 20 captives.
○ **D.** the children of enslaved Africans were also slaves.

B. Hiking is a great way to exercise. On a hike you can enjoy beautiful scenery, observe interesting plants and animals, and build your muscles—especially if you walk uphill. But hiking can be dangerous, if you're not careful.

First, you should plan your hiking trip. Carry a good map and make sure you have comfortable shoes with thick soles. It's smart to carry water, and food too, if it's going to be a long hike. Finally, set a comfortable walking pace. Going too fast will tire you out quickly.

Being prepared makes hiking less dangerous and more fun. So lace up those hiking boots and pack up your knapsack. There's a lot of beautiful countryside out there.

1. What is the best title for this story?
○ **A.** "How to Hike Safely"
○ **B.** "Good Hiking Shoes"
○ **C.** "Hiking Trails in Your Area"
○ **D.** "Where to Buy a Hiking Map"

2. Which of these is an *opinion*?
○ **A.** Hiking can build muscles.
○ **B.** Walking too fast can tire you out.
○ **C.** Hiking is the best way to exercise.
○ **D.** Tight shoes can cause blisters.

3. When hiking, which would you do last?
○ **A.** Wear comfortable shoes
○ **B.** Pack food and water
○ **C.** Carry a map
○ **D.** Walk at a comfortable pace

C. During the 1960s, women were inspired by the civil-rights movement, as they watched African-Americans fight for equal rights. They realized that women did not have the same rights and opportunities as men did. So they started the women's movement. The Civil Rights Act of 1964 was a big victory. That law made it illegal to discriminate against anyone because of skin color, religion, or gender.

Today, many women still choose the important job of caring for their families full-time. But now, women also make up almost half of the U.S. workforce. Women are moving into jobs that were never open to them before. They have become astronauts, construction workers, executives, engineers, and firefighters. But there is still no law that says that a woman must be guaranteed the same salary as a man who does the same job. Unfortunately, many women are paid less.

1. Why was the women's movement started?
○ **A.** Some women didn't have families.
○ **B.** Women had too many rights.
○ **C.** Women wanted to work.
○ **D.** Women wanted the same rights and opportunities as men.

2. Which happened last?
○ **A.** The Civil Rights Act was passed.
○ **B.** Women realized that they did not have the same rights as men.
○ **C.** The civil-rights movement started.
○ **D.** Women became almost half the workforce.

3. You can infer from this story that
○ **A.** women's lives have changed a lot over the last 30 years.
○ **B.** the civil-rights movement failed.
○ **C.** there are no female police officers or pilots.
○ **D.** few women care for their families full-time.

D.   Since ancient times, people all over the world have loved mountains. That's because mountains are some of the most beautiful landforms. They exist, in different shapes and sizes, on every continent.

Probably, the four best-known mountain ranges are the Himalayas in Asia, the Andes in South America, the Alps in Europe, and the Rockies in North America. All of these great ranges are different.

The Himalayas contain many of the world's tallest mountains, including Mount Everest—the tallest mountain in the world at 29,028 feet. In contrast, Mont Blanc, the tallest of the Alps, is only 15,771 feet. The Rockies are home to native North American wildlife such as bison and bighorn sheep, while many Andean peaks jut up from the *altiplano*—a vast, arid, high-altitude plain.

1. According to the article, how are the Alps different from the Himalayas?
○ **A.** The Alps are taller.
○ **B.** The Alps are more arid.
○ **C.** The Alps are smaller.
○ **D.** The Alps contain more wildlife.

2. Which of these is an *opinion*?
○ **A.** Mountains exist on every continent.
○ **B.** Mount Everest is 29,028 feet tall.
○ **C.** Mountains are beautiful landforms.
○ **D.** Bison live in the Rockies.

3. The main idea of this article is
○ **A.** only the Rockies contain wildlife.
○ **B.** people like the Alps much more than the Himalayas.
○ **C.** the Andes are less beautiful than the Rockies.
○ **D.** mountain ranges are beautiful and unique landforms.

4. What's the best title for this story?
○ **A.** "The World's Great Mountain Ranges"
○ **B.** "Life in Mountain Regions"
○ **C.** "Mount Everest and Mont Blanc"
○ **D.** "Wildlife in the Rockies"

E.   Once upon a time in India, a wise man named Sessa invented the game of chess. The maharaja, or king, liked this new game very much and said to Sessa, "Ask for anything in my kingdom and it shall be yours."

Sessa bowed his head. "Your Majesty," he said, "all I ask for is as many grains of rice as would fill the 64 squares of a chessboard, if one grain were put in the first square, two grains in the second, four in the third, eight in the fourth, and so on, doubling the number for each new square."

The king said, "Sessa, you deserve much more, but I will grant your **humble** request." A few days later, one of the maharaja's advisors said, "Your majesty, we cannot give Sessa his reward. The total amount of rice came to 18,446,744,073,709,551,615 grains! That's more rice than we have in the entire kingdom."

1. The purpose of this story is to
○ **A.** entertain.   ○ **C.** persuade.
○ **B.** advertise.   ○ **D.** protest.

2. In this story, **humble** means
○ **A.** small.   ○ **C.** grand.
○ **B.** shallow.   ○ **D.** bold.

3. According to the story, how many grains of rice go in the fourth square of the chessboard?
○ **A.** two   ○ **C.** eight
○ **B.** four   ○ **D.** twelve

4. You can conclude from this story that
○ **A.** the maharaja had Sessa thrown into prison.
○ **B.** Sessa knew something about math.
○ **C.** chess is not popular in India today.
○ **D.** ancient Indians didn't grow rice.

VOCABULARY
Which Word Is Missing?

In each of the following paragraphs, a word is missing. First, read each paragraph. Then choose the missing word from the list beneath the paragraph. Fill in the circle next to the word that is missing.

Sample:

Curtis likes his room to be _____. He puts his clothes away, makes his bed, and keeps papers piled neatly on his desk.

- ○ **A.** messy
- ○ **B.** smart
- ○ **C.** tidy
- ○ **D.** shy

1. The problem of endangered _____ is very serious. Unless we act now, many plants and animals could become extinct.

- ○ **A.** areas
- ○ **C.** pets
- ○ **B.** species
- ○ **D.** spires

2. Although the problem is _____, we shouldn't let its size keep us from taking action.

- ○ **A.** miniature
- ○ **C.** formidable
- ○ **B.** resolute
- ○ **D.** reliable

3. According to _____, there are several reasons why animals and plants become endangered. These experts should know. They study the delicate balance between life and the environment.

- ○ **A.** ecologists
- ○ **C.** zookeepers
- ○ **B.** engineers
- ○ **D.** gardeners

4. Animals become endangered when their _____ is drastically changed or destroyed. Humans are often the cause.

- ○ **A.** echo
- ○ **C.** family
- ○ **B.** habitat
- ○ **D.** hazard

5. If people around the world _____, we can help protect these plants and animals. But we must work together.

- ○ **A.** muster
- ○ **C.** manipulate
- ○ **B.** pledge
- ○ **D.** cooperate

6. Did you know that _____ plays a large part in many highway accidents? That's because people often keep driving even though they are tired. This can be as dangerous as driving drunk.

- ○ **A.** finance
- ○ **C.** destiny
- ○ **B.** fatigue
- ○ **D.** depression

7. When doing _____ driving, people should plan to stop, stretch, and rest every few hours. It's worth the extra time it takes to make these stops because they can help keep drivers alert.

- ○ **A.** long-dead
- ○ **C.** long-distance
- ○ **B.** long-handled
- ○ **D.** long-legged

8. Many accidents happen because people fall asleep at the wheel. You might be surprised to learn that it happens all the time. In fact, it's a fairly common _____.

- ○ **A.** occurrence
- ○ **C.** interruption
- ○ **B.** mechanism
- ○ **D.** priority

9. When tired, a driver's reactions can become _____. Stopping for a cup of coffee, soda, or tea can help drivers stay alert and react to things faster.

- ○ **A.** sluggish
- ○ **C.** noticeable
- ○ **B.** somber
- ○ **D.** ferocious

10. Tired drivers should continue on to the nearest rest area or other facility. They shouldn't pull their _____ onto the side of the road, as this is very dangerous. To stay awake while driving to a rest area, drivers should open the window for fresh air or play lively music on the radio.

- ○ **A.** throttles
- ○ **C.** vehicles
- ○ **B.** collisions
- ○ **D.** technicians

READING COMPREHENSION

Read each story. Then fill in the circle that best completes each sentence or answers each question.

What do you get when you cross a camel with a llama? The answer is not the punchline of a new joke. It's actually a new animal called a cama. Llamas produce nice wool, but camels are bigger. So scientists hope the cama will be a big wool producer!

1. A cama is
- ○ **A.** a small camel.
- ○ **B.** a cross between a camel and a llama.
- ○ **C.** a very special type of llama.
- ○ **D.** a new animal that lays eggs.

2. What is one difference between camels and llamas?
- ○ **A.** Camels are meaner.
- ○ **B.** Llamas are taller.
- ○ **C.** Camels are bigger.
- ○ **D.** Llamas don't produce wool.

A. How would you feel if you never saw a saguaro cactus again? You might not care, but the lesser long-nosed bats that depend on saguaro cactus blossoms for food sure would. They thrive on the cantaloupe-scented, cream-white blossoms that open each night to the desert air.

The Gila Woodpecker and the Gilded Flicker would care a lot as well. Both of these birds drill small holes in cactus trunks for their homes.

Without bats to pollinate them, the cactus can't reproduce. Ten types of bats that feed on cactus blossoms are already extinct. The lesser long-nosed bat is on the endangered list. Scientists are afraid the saguaro cactus is not far behind.

1. Why can't the cactus reproduce?
- ○ **A.** The bats that pollinate them are extinct or endangered.
- ○ **B.** Too many birds drill holes in the cactus for homes.
- ○ **C.** The lesser long-nosed bat eats all the cactus blossoms.
- ○ **D.** The cactus blossoms don't contain the pollen needed to reproduce.

2. The next paragraph is likely to be about
- ○ **A.** other endangered species.
- ○ **B.** how people are trying to save the cactus.
- ○ **C.** different birds of the desert.
- ○ **D.** the many different scents of cactus blossoms.

B.   In 2028, when the new millennium is over a quarter-century old, an asteroid is expected to whiz past Earth. But despite early reports, there's no need to worry. The closest it will come is 600,000 miles—more than twice as far away as the moon.

Asteroids are large rocks that revolve around the sun between the orbits of Mars and Jupiter. Some are as small as a TV set. Others are as wide as the length of California. At one-mile wide, the asteroid passing by earth in 2028 is medium-size.

First reports said the asteroid could come close enough to possibly hit the Earth—an event that could cause deadly tidal waves and climate problems. Fortunately, new information has shown that the Earth is definitely not in danger.

I. What is the best title for this story?
- ○ **A.** "Not a Close Call"
- ○ **B.** "The End of the Earth"
- ○ **C.** "How Asteroids Are Formed"
- ○ **D.** "Life in 2028"

2. How close will the asteroid pass to Earth?
- ○ **A.** closer than the moon
- ○ **B.** 400,000 miles
- ○ **C.** as close as Mars
- ○ **D.** 600,000 miles

3. According to the story, which of the following might happen if the asteroid hit Earth?
- ○ **A.** a world war
- ○ **B.** forest fires
- ○ **C.** tidal waves
- ○ **D.** famine

C.   At 7:00 a.m. (Nepalese time) on May 27, 1998, Tom Whittaker fulfilled the dream of his life. After a grueling eight-hour trek up **treacherous** rock and ice, Whittaker made it to the top of the world. He had climbed Mount Everest!

Whittaker was no ordinary climber. He lost his right foot and kneecap in a car accident in 1979. When he reached Mount Everest's summit, he became the first disabled person ever to successfully scale the world's tallest peak. Not bad for someone who days before was told by doctors he'd die if he didn't give up his climb—and his dream.

But, after considering the doctors' advice carefully, Whittaker and his team decided to keep going for their dream. So on a May morning, Whittaker stood at 29,028 feet (8848 meters)—literally on top of the world. What was he thinking? "Thank God there's no more up in front of me!"

I. What did Tom Whittaker do?
- ○ **A.** He became the first disabled person to climb Mount Everest.
- ○ **B.** He survived the world's worst car accident.
- ○ **C.** He climbed Mount Everest without permission.
- ○ **D.** He climbed Mount Everest without a team or other supporters.

2. In this story the word **treacherous** means
- ○ **A.** dangerous.
- ○ **B.** mean.
- ○ **C.** freezing.
- ○ **D.** wonderful.

3. You can infer from this story that
- ○ **A.** Tom Whittaker doesn't know how to climb.
- ○ **B.** Tom's doctors are very good.
- ○ **C.** Tom Whittaker is a very determined person.
- ○ **D.** Mount Everest is very easy to climb.

D. In 1918, the Spanish Influenza (flu) virus killed at least 20 million people, including 500,000 Americans. This 10-month flu epidemic was one of the worst natural disasters in history.

Since then, scientists have tried to answer a simple question: Why was that type of flu so deadly? Scientists wanted to study the flu's genetic structure for answers. But samples of the virus disappeared after the epidemic ended in 1919.

Now, scientists may be able to find answers after all. Government researchers found a small piece of lung tissue taken from a soldier who died of the flu in 1918 and completed genomic sequencing, or decoding, of the virus in 2005. They hope it will provide more information.

Their research is not just for history books. That flu virus—or one like it—may strike again sometime in the future. By knowing more, scientists can prepare to fight it and save lives.

l. How many people did the Spanish flu kill?
- ○ **A.** 18 million
- ○ **B.** 19 million
- ○ **C.** 20 million
- ○ **D.** 500,000

2. Why are scientists researching the Spanish flu?
- ○ **A.** to become famous
- ○ **B.** to get in history books
- ○ **C.** to be prepared if it shows up again
- ○ **D.** to find out why so few Americans died from it

3. The purpose of this article is to
- ○ **A.** protest.
- ○ **B.** inform.
- ○ **C.** persuade.
- ○ **D.** advertise.

4. What is the best title for this story?
- ○ **A.** "Spanish Flu: The Search for Answers"
- ○ **B.** "The Benefits of Scientific Research"
- ○ **C.** "Epidemics in History"
- ○ **D.** "An Unknown Soldier"

E. This excerpt is from an essay by Lauren Gleason, 13.

"Sometimes, the strangest things can be your friend." So my Grandma once said. Until now, I never understood what she meant. I have a best friend, but it is not another girl to giggle with. My friend cannot make me up to look like a movie star, curl luscious **locks** into my hair, or be the holder of my deepest, darkest secrets. Nor is my friend a dog, a loyal companion that follows its master far and wide and depends on him as a kitten does its mother for milk.

The thing where I go to seek friendship (for it never tells a lie and is always there) is a rickety, old porch swing that hangs from my porch roof by rusted chains hooked to oversize screws. Its wooden seat is just long enough for me to stretch my whole body out upon. The grains in the wood ripple in all directions, creating odd, circle-shaped figures. I always pay a visit to the swing when I'm lonely, angry, worried, or upset."

l. In this story, **locks** means
- ○ **A.** strands.
- ○ **B.** bows.
- ○ **C.** colors.
- ○ **D.** flowers.

2. The best description of the porch swing is
- ○ **A.** sparkling and new.
- ○ **B.** old and decrepit.
- ○ **C.** clean and shiny.
- ○ **D.** safe and well-maintained.

3. When does the author visit the swing?
- ○ **A.** when she's happy
- ○ **B.** to do her homework
- ○ **C.** after dinner
- ○ **D.** when she's upset

VOCABULARY

Synonyms

Read the underlined word in each phrase.
Mark the word below it that has the same
(or close to the same) meaning.

Sample:

   grave <u>consequence</u>
- ○ **A.** action
- ○ **B.** result
- ○ **C.** consent
- ○ **D.** solution

1. <u>customary</u> procedure
   - ○ **A.** normal
   - ○ **B.** strange
   - ○ **C.** precise
   - ○ **D.** follow

2. formidable <u>foe</u>
   - ○ **A.** friend
   - ○ **B.** obstacle
   - ○ **C.** task
   - ○ **D.** enemy

3. <u>illuminate</u> the building
   - ○ **A.** shut down
   - ○ **B.** fix up
   - ○ **C.** light up
   - ○ **D.** turn off

4. sharp <u>talons</u>
   - ○ **A.** tongues
   - ○ **B.** edges
   - ○ **C.** claws
   - ○ **D.** teeth

5. <u>muster</u> people
   - ○ **A.** gather
   - ○ **B.** help
   - ○ **C.** mollify
   - ○ **D.** quiet

6. <u>toxic</u> substance
   - ○ **A.** nutritious
   - ○ **B.** added
   - ○ **C.** poisonous
   - ○ **D.** bitter

7. <u>considerate</u> behavior
   - ○ **A.** rude
   - ○ **B.** thoughtful
   - ○ **C.** aggressive
   - ○ **D.** meek

Antonyms

Read the underlined word in each phrase.
Mark the word below it that means the
opposite or nearly the opposite.

Sample:

   <u>dejected</u> expression
- ○ **A.** sad
- ○ **B.** happy
- ○ **C.** angry
- ○ **D.** sorrowful

1. <u>evident</u> difference
   - ○ **A.** obvious
   - ○ **B.** unnoticeable
   - ○ **C.** unmentionable
   - ○ **D.** unlikely

2. <u>glum</u> look
   - ○ **A.** sad
   - ○ **B.** gleeful
   - ○ **C.** troubled
   - ○ **D.** unhappy

3. <u>meek</u> person
   - ○ **A.** aggressive
   - ○ **B.** polite
   - ○ **C.** creative
   - ○ **D.** dangerous

4. <u>overcast</u> day
   - ○ **A.** rainy
   - ○ **B.** dark
   - ○ **C.** sunny
   - ○ **D.** snowy

5. <u>torment</u> him
   - ○ **A.** torture
   - ○ **B.** soothe
   - ○ **C.** obey
   - ○ **D.** insult

6. <u>impulsive</u> action
   - ○ **A.** spontaneous
   - ○ **B.** considered
   - ○ **C.** unwise
   - ○ **D.** intelligent

7. <u>festive</u> occasion
   - ○ **A.** official
   - ○ **B.** unplanned
   - ○ **C.** cheerful
   - ○ **D.** somber

Reading Skills Practice Test 9

READING COMPREHENSION

Read each story. Then fill in the circle that best completes each sentence or answers each question.

SAMPLE

The World Series is baseball's biggest event. Each year, fans **applaud** the winners. When the Boston Red Sox won in 2002, fans applauded even more than usual. Pitcher Jon Lester's performance was nothing short of amazing. Earlier that year, doctors treated Lester for cancer. Not only did he beat cancer, but he battled back to become the World Series' winning pitcher.

1. In this passage the word **applaud** means
    ○ **A.** cheer for.
    ○ **B.** remember.
    ○ **C.** award.
    ○ **D.** fulfill.

2. What is the best title for this story?
    ○ **A.** "Champions of the World Series"
    ○ **B.** "Jon Lester's Incredible Victory"
    ○ **C.** "Baseball Winners"
    ○ **D.** "Jon Lester's Fastball"

A. In some places, fishermen use cyanide to catch fish. Cyanide is a deadly poison. Fishermen dump cyanide into the ocean, stunning big fish. The fish float to the surface where they are easy to catch. Unfortunately, cyanide fishing is a disaster for the environment.

Cyanide doesn't just stun fish; it kills the coral reefs on which fish live. Reefs are one of the most beautiful of all ecosystems. They take centuries to grow, so the damage caused by cyanide lasts for years. Without the coral, many ocean fish lose food sources and nesting grounds. With less coral, there will be fewer fish. In effect, the fishermen are poisoning their own future.

1. Why do some fishermen use cyanide?
    ○ **A.** They want to kill coral.
    ○ **B.** Cyanide makes it easy to catch big fish.
    ○ **C.** They are trying to rebuild damaged reefs.
    ○ **D.** It's the only way they can catch fish.

2. Which of these is an *opinion*?
    ○ **A.** Coral reefs take centuries to grow.
    ○ **B.** Cyanide use will soon be stopped.
    ○ **C.** Reefs are one of the most beautiful of all ecosystems.
    ○ **D.** In some places, fishermen use cyanide to catch fish.

B. Albert Einstein was born in Germany in 1879. As a child, few people guessed that he was going to be a famous scientist whose theories would change the world. He was slow in school, and some teachers thought he wasn't very bright.

When he grew up, Einstein wanted to be a science teacher—but nobody would hire him. He didn't give up, however, and went on to develop ideas about time and energy that changed science. One theory explained the way light beams travel, which made TV possible!

Einstein won the Nobel prize in 1921. In 1933 he fled from Nazi Germany and came to America. Here, he worked on atomic energy with other scientists. Although the atom bomb helped the U.S. end World War II, Einstein was always against using atomic energy to harm people. After the war, he worked for international peace.

1. Which of these is an *opinion* about Einstein?
- ○ **A.** He was born in Germany.
- ○ **B.** He worked on atomic energy.
- ○ **C.** He won the Nobel prize.
- ○ **D.** He wasn't very bright.

2. Which of these events occurred last?
- ○ **A.** Einstein won the Nobel prize.
- ○ **B.** Einstein worked on atomic energy with scientists in America.
- ○ **C.** Einstein fled Nazi Germany.
- ○ **D.** Einstein worked for international peace.

3. Einstein fled Germany because
- ○ **A.** he couldn't get a job.
- ○ **B.** he wanted to be a science teacher.
- ○ **C.** of the Nazis.
- ○ **D.** of the atomic bomb.

C. People who live in Death Valley definitely know the meaning of the word hot. In summer, they wear gloves to avoid frying their fingers on car door handles. To keep candles from melting, they store them in their refrigerators. Some folks here even give their babies ice cubes for toys. That's because they live in the hottest and lowest spot in the Western Hemisphere!

Death Valley lies 282 feet below sea level and can get as hot as 134 degrees Fahrenheit in the summer. It gets so hot that rain evaporates even before it touches the ground! Not that there is much rain to worry about in Death Valley. The bone-dry valley gets less than two inches of rainfall a year.

Despite its grim name, Death Valley contains 900 kinds of plants. There are also lots of animals. Bobcats, coyotes, and reptiles hide in the sand during the sweltering heat of the day and come out at night when it gets cooler.

1. You can guess that in Death Valley
- ○ **A.** plants don't need much rain.
- ○ **B.** animals don't need much food.
- ○ **C.** people avoid driving cars.
- ○ **D.** the temperature never drops below 100.

2. Bobcats, coyotes, and reptiles hide in the sand
- ○ **A.** to avoid people.
- ○ **B.** to avoid cars.
- ○ **C.** because of the rain.
- ○ **D.** because of the heat.

3. The main idea of this story is that
- ○ **A.** people shouldn't live in Death Valley.
- ○ **B.** there are 900 kinds of plants in Death Valley.
- ○ **C.** Death Valley is the lowest spot in the Western Hemisphere.
- ○ **D.** Death Valley is incredibly hot.

D. The next time you pass the candy aisle in the grocery store, stop for a moment and think about how each candy got invented. Who decided to make that candy cherry-tangerine flavored, or this one wild-berry surprise?

Chances are, it was a candy chemist. Candy chemists invent new flavors of candy. And while it may be fun, it's not that easy. They have over 2000 different ingredients to taste and work with. The pressure is on to come up with new and inventive flavors that are also delicious.

A surprising number of ingredients go into a flavor of candy. As they search for that perfect ingredient mix, candy chemists come face-to-face with the hardest part of their job. They have to eat all of their rejects!

I. What do candy chemists do?
- ○ **A.** They stock the candy aisles in supermarkets.
- ○ **B.** They invent new flavors of candy.
- ○ **C.** They eat a lot of candy and choose a favorite.
- ○ **D.** They search for the perfect candy.

2. Which of these is an *opinion*?
- ○ **A.** A candy chemist's job is not easy.
- ○ **B.** Candy chemists work with over 2000 ingredients.
- ○ **C.** Candy chemists must come up with new and delicious flavors.
- ○ **D.** A lot of ingredients go into a flavor of candy.

3. A good title for this story is
- ○ **A.** "My Favorite Flavor of Candy"
- ○ **B.** "200 Ingredients"
- ○ **C.** "Candy Chemists: A Sweet Job"
- ○ **D.** "A Look at a Supermarket Aisle"

E. When Prakesh first saw the bicycle in the store window, he couldn't believe it. It looked just like the one in the magazine he had seen back home in India. Somehow, seeing it made him realize he was **destined** to have this bike.

He began figuring out how long it would take him to buy it. The bike cost $499. He made $40 a week working part time for his uncle at the restaurant. He already had $120 in the bank. That meant he could buy the bike in 10 weeks. But what if someone else bought it first? Prakesh decided to see if the store would put it on layaway for him.

When he asked, the store clerk just smiled at him. "There's more than one of those bikes. I can order one for you at any time," he told Prakesh. "Why don't you let me know about two weeks before you have all the money. I'll order the bike for you then."

Prakesh couldn't wait. In just a few weeks he would be biking all over town!

I. In this story, **destined** means
- ○ **A.** fated.
- ○ **B.** unable.
- ○ **C.** not allowed.
- ○ **D.** sorry.

2. How much did Prakesh earn at his job each week?
- ○ **A.** $120
- ○ **B.** $499
- ○ **C.** $12
- ○ **D.** $40

3. You can infer from this article that Prakesh
- ○ **A.** had wanted a bike for a very long time.
- ○ **B.** didn't work very hard at his job.
- ○ **C.** didn't know how to ride a bike.
- ○ **D.** didn't like working at his uncle's restaurant.

VOCABULARY

Synonyms

Read the underlined word in each phrase.
Mark the word below it that has the same
(or close to the same) meaning.

Sample:

propose a plan
- A. reveal
- B. reject
- C. deny
- D. suggest

I. heavy luggage
- A. weight
- B. clothing
- C. load
- D. baggage

2. holiday fiesta
- A. party
- B. gift
- C. time
- D. spirit

3. speedy getaway
- A. path
- B. automobile
- C. escape
- D. gateway

4. humiliating experience
- A. merciless
- B. unique
- C. unusual
- D. embarrassing

5. endless quest
- A. fountain
- B. search
- C. story
- D. prank

6. acute pain
- A. dull
- B. minor
- C. sharp
- D. sudden

7. predicted storm
- A. understood
- B. foreseen
- C. unforeseen
- D. intense

Antonyms

Read the underlined word in each phrase.
Mark the word below it that means the
opposite or nearly the opposite.

Sample:

gleeful noises
- A. sad
- B. foreign
- C. sudden
- D. loud

I. hostile crowd
- A. savage
- B. friendly
- C. obedient
- D. humble

2. foster learning
- A. support
- B. allow
- C. encourage
- D. discourage

3. radiant colors
- A. glowing
- B. light
- C. dull
- D. bright

4. clammy cave
- A. hidden
- B. under the earth
- C. cold and windy
- D. hot and dry

5. abstract concept
- A. unoriginal
- B. original
- C. concrete
- D. exceptional

6. precious metal
- A. rare
- B. valuable
- C. soft
- D. common

7. imprecise answer
- A. exact
- B. uncertain
- C. thoughtless
- D. vague

Reading Skills Practice Test 10

READING COMPREHENSION

Read each story. Then fill in the circle that best completes each sentence or answers each question.

SAMPLE

Some zookeepers at Chicago's Lincoln Park Zoo have second jobs. They're also nannies—to baby orangutans, that is! When an orangutan mom can't care for her baby, "zoo nannies" lend **assistance**. The nannies treat a baby orangutan the way its mother would in the wild. The nannies wear fuzzy vests that feel like ape hair. They also swing the baby by its arms to carry it—just like an orangutan mom would.

1. The best title for this story is
  ○ **A.** "Zoo Nannies."
  ○ **B.** "Orangutan Moms."
  ○ **C.** "Ape Hair Vests."
  ○ **D.** "Carrying Baby Orangutans."

2. In this story, the word **assistance** means
  ○ **A.** money.
  ○ **B.** time.
  ○ **C.** hands.
  ○ **D.** help.

A. How far back can you trace your family tree? If you were Adrian Targett, you could go back 300 generations!

Scientists have discovered that Targett is a direct descendant of Cheddar Man. That's the name given to a 9,000-year-old skeleton found in a cave in the town of Cheddar, England. (Yes, they make cheese there.) "I've been in the cave a few times," says Targett, "but I never realized it was home to one of my ancestors."

How did Targett discover Cheddar Man was his ancestor? Scientists tested Cheddar Man's DNA and then compared it to the DNA of people from the town. When they compared Cheddar Man's DNA with Targett's, they discovered the two men were related.

1. Which of these would be the best title for this passage?
  ○ **A.** "How to Make Cheddar"
  ○ **B.** "Cheddar Man's Modern Relative"
  ○ **C.** "How DNA Works"
  ○ **D.** "Cave Skeletons"

2. How did scientists discover that Cheddar Man and Targett are related?
  ○ **A.** They had both men make cheese.
  ○ **B.** They compared the men's bones.
  ○ **C.** They compared the men's DNA.
  ○ **D.** They discovered that both men lived in caves.

3. What is the purpose of this passage?
  ○ **A.** to inform you about Cheddar Man's descendant
  ○ **B.** to persuade you that cheddar is a great cheese
  ○ **C.** to entertain you with facts about Cheddar Man
  ○ **D.** to convince you that DNA is not reliable

B. New Beginnings

we haven't spoken in over a year
it kind of scares me that it doesn't matter as
much anymore
I went up the hill
there was this new girl from Boston planting
flowers where we used to sit
when I volunteered to help
she smiled and handed me some seeds with a
small shovel
she told me I could take some home with me
and I smiled at her
as I started to walk back
I stuffed my pockets full of new beginnings

by Jennifer Chiou

I. What does the poem's narrator do after she smiles at the girl?
- ○ **A.** She goes up the hill.
- ○ **B.** She gets some seeds.
- ○ **C.** She volunteers to help.
- ○ **D.** She starts to walk back.

2. In the poem, the seeds represent
- ○ **A.** flowers.
- ○ **B.** new beginnings.
- ○ **C.** old friends.
- ○ **D.** a garden.

3. You can guess from this poem that
- ○ **A.** The narrator and the girl are old friends.
- ○ **B.** The narrator doesn't like the new girl.
- ○ **C.** The narrator is dealing with the loss of a friendship.
- ○ **D.** There are no hills where the narrator lives.

C.

For years, the biggest airplane flying was Boeing's 747. In 2004, the Airbus Company built an even bigger aircraft. The A3XX, a double-decker plane, became known as a super-jumbo. That's because it was even bigger than other jumbo jets, like the 747, at the time.

The new superplane is a virtual city in the air. The A3XX can fly more than 550 people from coast to coast. The plane is so big that it can contain cafes, sleeping rooms, and even a gym. Just imagine exercising 30,000 feet in the air!

Not everyone is convinced that super jumbos like the A3XX are such a good idea. Critics say that passengers may not like being on such a big plane. The huge number of passengers can create all kinds of difficulties. How long, for example, does it take for so many passengers to get on board? And will airports need new designs to handle lots of these monster flying machines?

I. Some people think the A3XX isn't a good idea because
- ○ **A.** the Airbus Company built it.
- ○ **B.** it is a double-decker.
- ○ **C.** it is too small.
- ○ **D.** passengers may not like how big it is.

2. What is the best title for this story?
- ○ **A.** "Superplane!"
- ○ **B.** "A History of Flying"
- ○ **C.** "Exercising in the Air"
- ○ **D.** "Airports"

3. How is the A3XX different from the 747?
- ○ **A.** It is bigger.
- ○ **B.** It is smaller.
- ○ **C.** It doesn't carry passengers.
- ○ **D.** It doesn't use airports.

D.   Playing and sledding after a snowstorm may be fun, but blizzards are serious business. Every year, people die when blizzards hit certain parts of the country. But you can beat a blizzard's **hazards** by being prepared. Before a blizzard hits, you should:

- Stock up on food and supplies. Don't forget batteries. Blizzards often knock the power out.
- Help your parents get those snow shovels and snowblowers out!
- Listen to the weather forecasts. Stay off the roads if a storm is about to hit.

Once a blizzard hits, if you do go outside remember to:

- Dress in layers. This helps to keep you warm by trapping your body's heat.
- Offer to help any elderly people you know by shoveling snow or getting supplies for them.
- Go inside the second you feel numb or sleepy.

1.   In this story, the word **hazards** means
- ○ **A.** aspects.
- ○ **B.** dangers.
- ○ **C.** snowdrifts.
- ○ **D.** cold.

2.   When should you stock up on supplies?
- ○ **A.** before the blizzard
- ○ **B.** during the blizzard
- ○ **C.** after the blizzard
- ○ **D.** never

3.   Based upon this story, which of the following statements would you agree with?
- ○ **A.** Preparing for a blizzard isn't important.
- ○ **B.** Blizzards are more serious than regular snowstorms.
- ○ **C.** Blizzards are never deadly.
- ○ **D.** Blizzards only happen in the Arctic.

E.   It happened during the 1998 Goodwill Games in Long Island, New York. Sang Lan, a gymnast from China and the Chinese national vaulting champion, was practicing the vault. Like a thousand times before, she **launched** her body into the air, but somehow, this time, she lost control. Hurtling forward, she crashed to the floor, head first.

The accident injured Sang's spinal cord, paralyzing her from the chest down. Confronted with such a life-changing event, Sang approached it the way she had gymnastics—by working hard. She began relearning life's basic skills. She had to learn simple actions all over again. Things that most of us never think about, like getting dressed or eating, were major tasks.

But Sang never looks back with anger or sorrow. Instead, she applied herself to her new goals: getting a college degree and becoming an advocate for the disabled. And in 2014, Sang also became a mother.

Says Sang, "When I had just gotten injured, I did think, 'What would I be doing if I hadn't got hurt?' But now I don't think about it. Regrets are pointless."

1.   In this story, the word **launched** means
- ○ **A.** hurtled.   ○ **C.** stepped.
- ○ **B.** rolled.   ○ **D.** relaxed.

2.   What was one of Sang's new goals in life?
- ○ **A.** eating
- ○ **B.** getting dressed
- ○ **C.** getting a college degree
- ○ **D.** going back to gymnastics

3.   The author wants you to see Sang as
- ○ **A.** determined.   ○ **C.** scared.
- ○ **B.** unhappy.   ○ **D.** regretful.

4.   What is the best title for this story?
- ○ **A.** "Vaulting"
- ○ **B.** "Gymnastics Accidents"
- ○ **C.** "One Gymnast's Courage"
- ○ **D.** "Life in China"

VOCABULARY

Synonyms

Read the underlined word in each phrase. Mark the word below it that has the same (or close to the same) meaning.

Sample:

swivel around
- ○ **A.** look
- ○ **B.** turn
- ○ **C.** fly
- ○ **D.** float

I. contribute aid
- ○ **A.** purchase
- ○ **B.** donate
- ○ **C.** redeem
- ○ **D.** accept

2. clash of ideas
- ○ **A.** collision
- ○ **B.** failure
- ○ **C.** ruin
- ○ **D.** downpour

3. revive hope
- ○ **A.** survive
- ○ **B.** reject
- ○ **C.** recover
- ○ **D.** provide

4. shapeless being
- ○ **A.** shapely
- ○ **B.** formless
- ○ **C.** square
- ○ **D.** strange

5. flurry of activity
- ○ **A.** burst
- ○ **B.** end
- ○ **C.** halt
- ○ **D.** lack

6. tranquil seas
- ○ **A.** wavy
- ○ **B.** wet
- ○ **C.** calm
- ○ **D.** cold

7. menacing dog
- ○ **A.** threatening
- ○ **B.** furry
- ○ **C.** friendly
- ○ **D.** large

Antonyms

Read the underlined word in each phrase. Mark the word below it that means the opposite or nearly the opposite.

Sample:

carefree attitude
- ○ **A.** unbelievable
- ○ **B.** laughing
- ○ **C.** happy
- ○ **D.** serious

I. clammy grip
- ○ **A.** cold
- ○ **B.** firm
- ○ **C.** icy and wet
- ○ **D.** warm and dry

2. gleeful yell
- ○ **A.** joyous
- ○ **B.** nervous
- ○ **C.** loud
- ○ **D.** unhappy

3. typical reaction
- ○ **A.** usual
- ○ **B.** unusual
- ○ **C.** tired
- ○ **D.** meaningless

4. create chaos
- ○ **A.** order
- ○ **B.** disorder
- ○ **C.** action
- ○ **D.** understanding

5. hostile crowd
- ○ **A.** horrid
- ○ **B.** futile
- ○ **C.** hysterical
- ○ **D.** friendly

6. purchase clothing
- ○ **A.** shop
- ○ **B.** carry
- ○ **C.** take
- ○ **D.** sell

7. tardy arrival
- ○ **A.** skinny
- ○ **B.** kind
- ○ **C.** early
- ○ **D.** late

READING COMPREHENSION

Read each story. Then fill in the circle that best completes each sentence or answers each question.

On the morning of November 14, 1963, the crew on a fishing boat off the coast of Iceland watched an unusual birth — the birth of an island! A dark smoky mass rose out of the water from a volcano that was erupting beneath the ocean. The new island was named Surtsey. Even today, it continues to grow from erupting lava.

1. What is the best title for this story?
- ○ **A.** "Volcanoes and Earthquakes"
- ○ **B.** "An Island Is Born"
- ○ **C.** "The People of Iceland"
- ○ **D.** "Iceland's Fishing Industry"

2. From the story, you can infer that
- ○ **A.** lava forms some islands.
- ○ **B.** Iceland is a volcanic island.
- ○ **C.** volcanoes can form anywhere.
- ○ **D.** the fishing boat's owner was named Surtsey.

A.   Around 450 years ago, a baker in an Italian village put some tomatoes on flattened bread and called his creation pizza. Two hundred years later, someone added cheese. No one knows when pepperoni was first added. What we do know is that, today, Americans **consume** more than 30 million slices of pizza a day. And those are just the slices sold in restaurants!

Pizzas through the ages have had one thing in common: They are often baked directly on the hot floor of a stone oven. Why? The stone used in ovens is porous, or full of tiny holes. That means it can soak up water from the crust as the pizza bakes, so the pizza bottom gets crispy.

1. In this story, the word **consume** means
- ○ **A.** prepare.
- ○ **B.** sell.
- ○ **C.** make.
- ○ **D.** eat.

2. You can infer from this story that
- ○ **A.** the inventor of pizza became famous.
- ○ **B.** not all pizza is sold in restaurants.
- ○ **C.** most people don't like crispy pizza crusts.
- ○ **D.** people didn't like pizza before the cheese was added.

3. What causes a pizza crust to become crispy?
- ○ **A.** Cheese covers the crust.
- ○ **B.** Cheese absorbs water in the crust.
- ○ **C.** The stone oven absorbs water from the crust.
- ○ **D.** The stone oven releases water into the crust.

B. In New York State, some pesky critters may be playing a deadly trick on a Halloween treat. Scientists think that microbes, or bugs so small that they can't be seen without a microscope, are to blame for a strange disease cropping up in some pumpkin patches.

The disease clogs tiny vessels, or tubes, inside the pumpkins. These tubes carry water and nutrients. When the vessels are blocked, pumpkins can't get the **nourishment** they need. So they starve. Infected pumpkins lose their bright-orange color and eventually rot.

The mysterious disease has also been spotted in New York squash and cucumbers. But that doesn't mean people should start worrying about a vegetable shortage. The sick veggies are only a small percentage of the pumpkin, squash, and cucumber crops. So those who were secretly hoping for a few vegetable-free meals better get ready for second helpings instead.

1. In this article, the word **nourishment** means
   - ○ **A.** bugs.
   - ○ **B.** care.
   - ○ **C.** sunlight.
   - ○ **D.** food and water.

2. How does the disease kill pumpkins?
   - ○ **A.** It clogs vessels inside the pumpkins.
   - ○ **B.** It clogs the pumpkin plants' roots.
   - ○ **C.** It makes the pumpkins lose their orange color.
   - ○ **D.** It makes the pumpkins stop growing.

3. What do scientists think is causing the pumpkin disease?
   - ○ **A.** humans
   - ○ **B.** bad weather
   - ○ **C.** microbes
   - ○ **D.** insects

C. It's July and you have to mow the lawn. You grab your robot grass cutter and toss it in the backyard. Minutes later, the frisbee-shaped robot is nibbling away at the grass, and you're headed for the beach.

Yes, mowing the lawn is that simple, says Mark W. Tilden, a scientist who studies robots. Tilden shares his Los Alamos, New Mexico, home with more than 50 robots. His robotic roommates range from credit-card-sized floor cleaners to creatures that report on break-ins. Others wash windows, kill flies, and yes, cut the grass.

Tilden's robots don't rely on humans to power them. Instead, they draw energy from the sun, lamps, and televisions. Tilden constructs his robots from pieces of broken VCRs, computers, calculators, CD players, TVs, and toys—anything he can find. "All the parts you need to build a robot are sitting in the bottom of your junk drawer," he says. Whoever thought making robots could be that easy! Of course, you can also go out and buy one, too.

1. Tilden's robots draw energy from
   - ○ **A.** televisions.
   - ○ **B.** computers.
   - ○ **C.** VCRs.
   - ○ **D.** CD players.

2. Which of these is an *opinion*?
   - ○ **A.** Tilden's robots wash windows, kill flies, and cut the grass.
   - ○ **B.** Lawns will need mowing in July.
   - ○ **C.** Making robots is easy.
   - ○ **D.** Tilden shares his New Mexico home with more than 50 robots.

3. You can guess from this story that
   - ○ **A.** Tilden thinks robots are boring.
   - ○ **B.** Tilden thinks robots are really cool.
   - ○ **C.** Robots wouldn't be very good at mowing the lawn.
   - ○ **D.** Robots require lots of unique parts.

D.   One of the most spectacular sights in China isn't a city, a snow-capped peak, or a desert sand dune. It's a wall! To be more **precise**, it's the Great Wall, an ancient structure that took thousands of workers more than 40 years to build.

Most of the Great Wall was built between 259 and 210 B.C., during the reign of Emperor Ch'in Shih Huang Ti. He was a powerful leader who united many small states into a strong empire. He built the wall to protect his empire against Mongol horsemen who swept down from the north, raiding villages and towns. At 25 feet tall and almost 4,000 miles long, the Great Wall of China is the longest structure ever built. That's 1,000 miles longer than the distance from the east coast of the United States to the west coast!

1.   Ch'in Shih Huang Ti built the wall to
○ **A.** keep people from escaping.
○ **B.** employ thousands of workers.
○ **C.** protect his empire.
○ **D.** unite China.

2.   In this story, the word **precise** means
○ **A.** exact.
○ **B.** bold.
○ **C.** serious.
○ **D.** sensible.

3.   You can infer from the story that
○ **A.** Ch'in Shih Huang Ti was nice.
○ **B.** the Great Wall is an important historical structure.
○ **C.** China has no sand dunes.
○ **D.** Mongols lived south of Ch'in Shih Huang Ti's empire.

E.   Imagine being able to switch on lights or television sets just by using your brain. It's not science fiction. Scientists in Australia are now testing an invention that could allow people to do just that!

How does it work? The human brain runs on tiny bits of electricity. When people are relaxed, most of the brain's electricity is a type called alpha waves. To capture brain power, scientists attach wires to people's heads and tell the people to relax. The wires pick up alpha waves and run them through a machine that makes the waves thousands of times stronger. Then the waves flick a switch that can control a light, a TV, an electric toy car, or other gadget. Experts hope this discovery will help disabled people who can't control switches with their hands.

1.   The main idea of this story is that
○ **A.** people are usually relaxed.
○ **B.** when people are relaxed, their brains produce alpha waves.
○ **C.** an invention may let the brain switch appliances on and off.
○ **D.** electricity travels in waves.

2.   Alpha waves are created when
○ **A.** people watch television.
○ **B.** people are disabled.
○ **C.** people are hooked up to wires.
○ **D.** people relax.

3.   You can guess from this story that
○ **A.** scientists are still perfecting this invention.
○ **B.** all animals make alpha waves.
○ **C.** most people cannot relax.
○ **D.** people watch a lot of TV.

4.   This story would probably go on to talk about
○ **A.** the remote control.
○ **B.** other brain-power experiments.
○ **C.** how alpha waves are created.
○ **D.** how televisions work.

VOCABULARY

Synonyms

Read the underlined word in each phrase. Mark the word below it that has the same (or close to the same) meaning.

Sample:

amble along
- ○ **A.** run
- ○ **B.** stroll
- ○ **C.** jog
- ○ **D.** skip

1. gnaw a bone
   - ○ **A.** chew
   - ○ **B.** swallow
   - ○ **C.** spit out
   - ○ **D.** lick

2. erect posture
   - ○ **A.** slumped
   - ○ **B.** upright
   - ○ **C.** bent
   - ○ **D.** slouching

3. former president
   - ○ **A.** current
   - ○ **B.** previous
   - ○ **C.** next
   - ○ **D.** future

4. vacant house
   - ○ **A.** occupied
   - ○ **B.** empty
   - ○ **C.** old
   - ○ **D.** big

5. reveal the truth
   - ○ **A.** show
   - ○ **B.** hide
   - ○ **C.** fight
   - ○ **D.** embrace

6. drastic measure
   - ○ **A.** extreme
   - ○ **B.** ineffective
   - ○ **C.** effective
   - ○ **D.** costly

7. sensitive child
   - ○ **A.** timid
   - ○ **B.** easily hurt
   - ○ **C.** tough
   - ○ **D.** quiet

Antonyms

Read the underlined word in each phrase. Mark the word below it that means the opposite or nearly the opposite.

Sample:

elegant clothes
- ○ **A.** casual
- ○ **B.** formal
- ○ **C.** new
- ○ **D.** old

1. pester someone
   - ○ **A.** meet
   - ○ **B.** contact
   - ○ **C.** bother
   - ○ **D.** ignore

2. lousy idea
   - ○ **A.** great
   - ○ **B.** terrible
   - ○ **C.** creative
   - ○ **D.** silly

3. vivid colors
   - ○ **A.** dull
   - ○ **B.** bright
   - ○ **C.** pastel
   - ○ **D.** loud

4. suitable outfit
   - ○ **A.** inappropriate
   - ○ **B.** perfect
   - ○ **C.** ugly
   - ○ **D.** coordinated

5. deny all charges
   - ○ **A.** admit
   - ○ **B.** laugh
   - ○ **C.** write
   - ○ **D.** spend

6. flammable cloth
   - ○ **A.** aflame
   - ○ **B.** flimsy
   - ○ **C.** fireproof
   - ○ **D.** stiff

7. homely appearance
   - ○ **A.** plain
   - ○ **B.** attractive
   - ○ **C.** ugly
   - ○ **D.** unattractive

Reading Skills Practice Test 12

READING COMPREHENSION

Read each story. Then fill in the circle that best completes each sentence or answers each question.

In his 20s, Tiger Woods was already being called one of the greatest athletes of our time. This **exceptional** golfer has broken numerous records. He's so famous that people use only his first name when they talk about him.

1. In this story the word **exceptional** means
- ○ **A.** accepting.
- ○ **B.** really talented.
- ○ **C.** precise.
- ○ **D.** young.

2. What is the best title for this story?
- ○ **A.** "Golf in America"
- ○ **B.** "Exceptional Athletes"
- ○ **C.** "The World's Most Famous Tiger"
- ○ **D.** "People Without Last Names"

A. The Vikings struck fear in the hearts of all who heard of them. These awesome warriors and masters of the sea stole, slashed, and burned their way through life. However, most of Europe hadn't heard of the Vikings before 793 A.A. That's when Viking warriors sailed to England and launched an attack on wealthy English monks. This was the beginning of 300 years of Viking domination of Northern Europe.

But the Vikings had a less bloodthirsty side, as well. They were amazing sailors and explorers, and one of them, Leif Eriksson, led a ship whose crew became the first Europeans to land in North America. They also settled the cold islands of Greenland and Iceland in the North Atlantic.

1. Most of Europe learned about the Vikings
- ○ **A.** 300 years ago.
- ○ **B.** 700 years ago.
- ○ **C.** when Vikings settled Greenland.
- ○ **D.** in 793 A.A.

2. The story would probably go on to discuss
- ○ **A.** Wildlife in Greenland and Iceland.
- ○ **B.** English monks.
- ○ **C.** Leif Eriksson's life.
- ○ **D.** the settlement of North America.

3. You can guess that the Vikings
- ○ **A.** were short.
- ○ **B.** were sometimes violent.
- ○ **C.** took over Europe.
- ○ **D.** were not very smart.

B.   Did you ever eat something that didn't agree with you? If you were a frog, it would not have been a problem. When frogs accidentally eat a poisonous insect, they get rid of it the hard way—they throw up their whole stomachs!

"Frogs aren't picky about what they swallow," explains biologist Richard Wassersug. "They take in a lot of food at one time, and sometimes they eat something **toxic**."

When this happens, a frog turns its stomach inside out and expels it through its esophagus (the tube that connects the mouth and stomach). The frog then wipes off the poison and swallows its stomach back down.

l. What is the best title for this story?
○ **A.** "How Frogs Deal With Upset Stomachs"
○ **B.** "Common Frog Poisons"
○ **C.** "Animal Stomachs"
○ **D.** "Frogs Have No Necks"

2. In this story, the word **toxic** means
○ **A.** delicious.
○ **B.** awful.
○ **C.** large.
○ **D.** poisonous.

3. What happens after a frog throws up its stomach?
○ **A.** It goes to sleep.
○ **B.** It grows another stomach.
○ **C.** It wipes off the poison.
○ **D.** It dies.

C.   Early in the 1800s, Japan wanted nothing to do with the outside world. Its policy of isolation dated to 1638. Before that, Japan had traded with European countries. But Japan's rulers feared that those countries might try to take over Japan, so they stopped the trading.

For two centuries, Japan was mostly cut off from the outside world. Its rulers allowed only limited trade with nearby Asian countries and with the Dutch.

During that time, foreign ships could not stop at Japanese ports—not even for food or fuel. Then, in 1853, U.S. Navy Commodore Matthew Perry negotiated with the Japanese and helped to open up the country. Today, Japan is one of the world's most technologically advanced societies, and its economy depends upon trade with other countries.

l. This story is mostly about
○ **A.** the history of trading in Japan.
○ **B.** modern technology in Japan.
○ **C.** different kinds of Japanese ships.
○ **D.** economies of Asian countries.

2. Why was Japan closed to the outside world?
○ **A.** They didn't have goods to trade.
○ **B.** Japan was too far away.
○ **C.** Japan's rulers were afraid Japan would be taken over.
○ **D.** Japan's rulers didn't like the Dutch.

3. You can conclude from this story that
○ **A.** Japan was taken over by Europe.
○ **B.** Japan was not taken over by Europe.
○ **C.** Dutch traders could speak Japanese.
○ **D.** the U.S. does not trade with Japan.

4. The purpose of this article is to
○ **A.** inform.
○ **B.** entertain.
○ **C.** persuade.
○ **D.** convince.

D.   Eighteen-year-old Billy Campbell was riding fast and hard. His horse was exhausted. Campbell hated to push the poor creature, but he was determined to make it to the next station faster than ever before.

He made it! Usually, Campbell liked to take a minute to relax at the station, but not this time. He grabbed his saddlebags and leaped off his horse. Seconds later, he and his precious cargo—news from the nation's capital—were on a new horse, continuing their journey west.

Campbell took part in a record-breaking feat in March 1861. That is when Pony Express riders carried the words of a speech by President Abraham Lincoln from St. Joseph, Missouri, to Sacramento, California, in 7 days and 17 hours. It was one of the most exciting rides ever!

1.   What was Campbell carrying?
- ○ **A.** a sidesaddle
- ○ **B.** medical supplies
- ○ **C.** food
- ○ **D.** a speech

2.   Which of these is an *opinion*?
- ○ **A.** Campbell had a very exciting ride.
- ○ **B.** Campbell carried saddlebags.
- ○ **C.** Campbell's horse was exhausted.
- ○ **D.** Campbell was traveling west.

3.   From this story you can guess that
- ○ **A.** mail should be delivered by horse.
- ○ **B.** Billy Campbell was not a good rider.
- ○ **C.** Lincoln's speech was very important.
- ○ **D.** Lincoln's speech was not important.

4.   What is the best title for this story?
- ○ **A.** "Special Delivery, 1861"
- ○ **B.** "Abe Lincoln"
- ○ **C.** "Horses"
- ○ **D.** "U.S. Mail"

E.   Other than natural-history museums, Antarctica is the best place to hunt for meteorites, or space rocks, that crash into Earth. Geologist Ralph Harvey and his team from ANSMET (the Antarctic Search for Meteorites) have found over 390 meteorites.

Why are so many meteorites found in Antarctica? Harvey says it's because Antarctica is a **vast** stretch of white ice and snow. Meteorites easily show up on such a surface.

Meteorites in Antarctica are first covered by layers of snow. Packed in under pressure, the snow turns to ice. Over thousands of years, the ice spreads out toward the edges of the continent and usually breaks off as icebergs. As the ice disappears, meteorites show up on the surface, just waiting to be found by the ANSMET team.

1.   According to the story, what happens first?
- ○ **A.** Icebergs break off.
- ○ **B.** Snow turns to ice.
- ○ **C.** Meteorites show up on the surface.
- ○ **D.** Meteorites are covered by snow.

2.   In this story, **vast** means
- ○ **A.** icy.   ○ **C.** cold.
- ○ **B.** rocky.   ○ **D.** large.

3.   How many meteorites has ANSMET found?
- ○ **A.** thousands
- ○ **B.** a few
- ○ **C.** over 390
- ○ **D.** less than 350

4.   You can guess from this story that
- ○ **A.** meteorites don't weigh very much.
- ○ **B.** Antarctica is cold.
- ○ **C.** many people live in Antarctica.
- ○ **D.** you can find meteorites only in Antarctica.

VOCABULARY

Synonyms

Read the underlined word in each phrase. Mark the word below it that has the same (or close to the same) meaning.

Sample:

fatal accident
- ○ **A.** bad
- ○ **B.** minor
- ○ **C.** deadly
- ○ **D.** traffic

1. afternoon excursion
   - ○ **A.** outing
   - ○ **B.** nap
   - ○ **C.** errand
   - ○ **D.** chore

2. tidy room
   - ○ **A.** neat
   - ○ **B.** messy
   - ○ **C.** large
   - ○ **D.** cluttered

3. gleeful cry
   - ○ **A.** miserable
   - ○ **B.** frightened
   - ○ **C.** scary
   - ○ **D.** happy

4. serene expression
   - ○ **A.** unhappy
   - ○ **B.** peaceful
   - ○ **C.** serious
   - ○ **D.** stern

5. muster the energy
   - ○ **A.** expend
   - ○ **B.** store up
   - ○ **C.** gather up
   - ○ **D.** release

6. abbreviate the word
   - ○ **A.** say
   - ○ **B.** shorten
   - ○ **C.** write
   - ○ **D.** lose

7. distribute papers
   - ○ **A.** read
   - ○ **B.** organize
   - ○ **C.** sell
   - ○ **D.** give out

Antonyms

Read the underlined word in each phrase. Mark the word below it that means the opposite or nearly the opposite.

Sample:

hostile reaction
- ○ **A.** friendly
- ○ **B.** mean
- ○ **C.** startled
- ○ **D.** crazy

1. rural area
   - ○ **A.** country
   - ○ **B.** farming
   - ○ **C.** urban
   - ○ **D.** coastal

2. pulled taut
   - ○ **A.** loose
   - ○ **B.** tight
   - ○ **C.** free
   - ○ **D.** down

3. drab appearance
   - ○ **A.** pale
   - ○ **B.** boring
   - ○ **C.** happy
   - ○ **D.** bright

4. lush surroundings
   - ○ **A.** barren
   - ○ **B.** luxurious
   - ○ **C.** rainy
   - ○ **D.** normal

5. vague answer
   - ○ **A.** whispered
   - ○ **B.** wrong
   - ○ **C.** specific
   - ○ **D.** careful

6. insert the key
   - ○ **A.** make
   - ○ **B.** turn
   - ○ **C.** put in
   - ○ **D.** take out

7. descend the mountain
   - ○ **A.** glimpse
   - ○ **B.** go down
   - ○ **C.** go up
   - ○ **D.** destroy

Reading Skills Practice Test 13

READING COMPREHENSION

Read each story. Then fill in the circle that best completes each sentence or answers each question.

SAMPLE

The hole in the ozone layer, a protective shield around our planet that blocks harmful sun rays, is bigger than ever. Ozone is a layer of gas in the stratosphere, a part of the atmosphere 7 to 31 miles above the Earth. Tests show that the hole over the South Pole is now about the size of North America. As the hole grows, there's more risk of getting severe sunburns, which can cause skin cancer.

I. According to the story, what is one effect of the growing hole in the ozone?
○ **A.** There is more risk of being poisoned by the stratosphere.
○ **B.** There's more risk of getting severe sunburns.
○ **C.** It rains more on Earth.
○ **D.** It rains less on Earth.

A. The peanut butter and jelly sandwich is an everyday food for some kids. But for other kids, the sandwich can be a killer. That's because some kids are highly allergic to peanuts. In severe cases, even the presence of peanut particles in the air can cause a life-threatening allergic reaction.

An estimated 5 million people in the United States suffer from food allergies, according to the Food Allergy Network. Of these, about 2 million are kids. And of all the allergies kids can have, peanuts are among the most dangerous. That's why many schools have taken anti-peanut measures.

Some schools just restrict the use of peanuts and peanut butter on campus. But other schools have taken the drastic step of banning peanut products altogether. That means absolutely no peanut butter and jelly sandwiches allowed!

I. Why shouldn't some kids eat peanut butter and jelly sandwiches?
○ **A.** They don't like peanut butter and jelly.
○ **B.** Peanut butter and jelly is fattening.
○ **C.** They are allergic to peanut butter.
○ **D.** They are allergic to jelly.

2. What is the best title for this story?
○ **A.** "Peanut Alert"
○ **B.** "A Great Sandwich Gone Bad"
○ **C.** "A History of Allergies"
○ **D.** "Peanuts Everywhere"

B. Many foster children are forced to move three or four times during their childhood years. When 13-year-old Aubyn Burnside learned that most of these kids had to use plastic garbage bags to move their **possessions** from place to place, she decided to do something about it.

Since she was 11 years old, Aubyn, of Hickory, North Carolina, has been collecting hundreds of suitcases for kids who were forced to leave their homes. "I think the suitcases give the children a little security and dignity," Aubyn says.

Aubyn began her suitcase collecting by posting signs at libraries, grocery stores, churches, and schools, asking for donations. In less than a year, Aubyn provided suitcases for 300 foster children in her county. Today, Aubyn's volunteer program, "Suitcases for Kids," provides luggage to foster children in all 50 states and Canada.

1. In this article, the word **possessions** means
  ○ **A.** clothes.
  ○ **B.** homework.
  ○ **C.** belongings.
  ○ **D.** brothers and sisters.

2. Which of these is an *opinion*?
  ○ **A.** Aubyn provided suitcases for 300 foster children in her county.
  ○ **B.** Many foster children are forced to move three or four times.
  ○ **C.** Suitcases give foster children a little security and dignity.
  ○ **D.** "Suitcases for Kids" provides luggage to foster children in all 50 states.

3. This story would probably go on to talk about
  ○ **A.** how luggage is made.
  ○ **B.** how foster kids feel about getting a suitcase.
  ○ **C.** how well Aubyn does in school.
  ○ **D.** what happens when foster children get adopted.

C. The safety bar clicks into place. You take a deep breath as the clanking wheels carry you slowly up the hill. Suddenly, you're plunging down at 80 miles per hour—holding on for dear life and screaming wildly.

If this is your idea of fun, then you're one of the millions of people willing to wait in 2-hour lines for a $2^1/_2$ minute roller-coaster ride at one of America's 600 theme parks. Roller coasters are more popular than ever, it seems.

Roller coasters have come a long way since they first appeared in Russia more than 500 years ago. For thrills, Russians rode sleighs down ice-covered wooden tracks. Since then, roller coasters have gotten a lot more sophisticated, but the basic idea remains the same. Most of them use the G-force, or the force of Earth's gravity, to move. Earth's gravity pulls at you with a force of 1G, but

most roller coasters are designed to pull with a greater force. Many now have a force of 4G–5G. The Tower of Terror in South Africa measures 6.3G! That makes for some heavy, and very scary, thrills.

1. How do roller coasters move?
  ○ **A.** They use the G-force.
  ○ **B.** They have engines.
  ○ **C.** They are battery powered.
  ○ **D.** They are pushed.

2. From this story you can guess that
  ○ **A.** people love the thrill of going fast.
  ○ **B.** the best roller coasters are in Russia.
  ○ **C.** most people don't like roller coasters.
  ○ **D.** Earth's gravity is very dangerous.

D.   Miles below the ocean's surface, **hydrothermal** vents spit out water hot enough to melt lead—650 degrees. These vents provide energy for tube worms, clams, and octopuses that live in the deepest depths of the sea. Boiling water from the vents contains chemicals that change into food for hundreds of unusual, and sometimes monstrous, deep-sea species.

Although oceans cover more than 70 percent of the Earth's surface, the depths of the sea remain largely unexplored. But recent discoveries are helping scientists uncover some of the ocean's mysteries. A colony of a fish species believed to be extinct was recently found, and scientists continue to seek out giant squids.

Few giant squids have been seen alive, but several dead ones have washed ashore. A giant squid's remains can stretch for 60 feet. Its arm is as thick as a man's leg, and its eyes are as big as hubcaps.

1. What have scientists recently found in the deep sea?
  ○ **A.** a live giant clam
  ○ **B.** a colony of fish thought to be extinct
  ○ **C.** a colony of sea monsters
  ○ **D.** a live giant octopus

2. In this story, the word **hydrothermal** means
  ○ **A.** cold water.
  ○ **B.** hot water.
  ○ **C.** giant.
  ○ **D.** tiny.

3. What is the main idea of this story?
  ○ **A.** Interesting things live at the bottom of our oceans.
  ○ **B.** The giant squid is an incredible creature.
  ○ **C.** Scientists don't really want to explore the oceans' depths.
  ○ **D.** It's always incredibly cold at the bottom of the ocean.

E.   Puerto Rico's El Yunque rain forest is the only rain forest in the U.S. national forest system. That's one reason to visit it. A better reason is that it's very beautiful.

More than 240 kinds of trees and 1,000 kinds of plants live in El Yunque. It also is home to over 60 kinds of birds. What makes it such a great home for these living things? It has a lot of water. El Yunque receives over 200 inches of rain each year. Plus, six major rivers trace their sources here.

Besides plants and animals, what else is there to see in El Yunque? There are several spectacular waterfalls, including La Coca Falls and La Mina Falls. And then there is the mountain of El Yunque itself. This mountain rises over 3,500 feet above sea level.

According to legend, El Yunque was the home of Yukiyú, the Taino Indians' protecting spirit. Tainos were the original inhabitants of Puerto Rico.

1. What makes El Yunque a great home for living things?
  ○ **A.** It has a big mountain.
  ○ **B.** It's in a great location.
  ○ **C.** It has a lot of water.
  ○ **D.** It's very cold all year-round.

2. The purpose of this story is to
  ○ **A.** describe the island of Puerto Rico.
  ○ **B.** explain how rain forests work.
  ○ **C.** persuade you to visit El Yunque.
  ○ **D.** tell the history of the Taino Indians.

3. This story would probably go on to talk about
  ○ **A.** the best time of year to visit El Yunque.
  ○ **B.** rain forests all over the world.
  ○ **C.** the birds of North America.
  ○ **D.** famous Puerto Ricans.

VOCABULARY

Synonyms

Read the underlined word in each phrase. Mark the word below it that has the same (or close to the same) meaning.

Sample:

feeling <u>drowsy</u>
- ○ **A.** awake
- ○ **B.** sleepy
- ○ **C.** unhappy
- ○ **D.** excited

I. <u>fabulous</u> clothes
- ○ **A.** great
- ○ **B.** awful
- ○ **C.** new
- ○ **D.** old

2. <u>needless</u> waste
- ○ **A.** enormous
- ○ **B.** little
- ○ **C.** unnecessary
- ○ **D.** necessary

3.. <u>swivel</u> quickly
- ○ **A.** leave
- ○ **B.** swim
- ○ **C.** turn
- ○ **D.** talk

4. <u>primary</u> problem
- ○ **A.** main
- ○ **B.** last
- ○ **C.** other
- ○ **D.** small

5. <u>wage</u> war
- ○ **A.** pay
- ○ **B.** make
- ○ **C.** win
- ○ **D.** lose

6. <u>bestow</u> a gift
- ○ **A.** give
- ○ **B.** take
- ○ **C.** tow
- ○ **D.** allow

7. <u>evident</u> problem
- ○ **A.** unlikely
- ○ **B.** obvious
- ○ **C.** unclear
- ○ **D.** unavoidable

Antonyms

Read the underlined word in each phrase. Mark the word below it that means the opposite or nearly the opposite.

Sample:

<u>exotic</u> fruit
- ○ **A.** tasty
- ○ **B.** sour
- ○ **C.** ordinary
- ○ **D.** popular

I. <u>panicky</u> feeling
- ○ **A.** calm
- ○ **B.** nervous
- ○ **C.** good
- ○ **D.** bad

2.. <u>merciless</u> enemy
- ○ **A.** evil
- ○ **B.** mean
- ○ **C.** compassionate
- ○ **D.** helpful

3. <u>formal</u> dinner
- ○ **A.** casual
- ○ **B.** unplanned
- ○ **C.** deluxe
- ○ **D.** expensive

4. <u>teeming</u> with ants
- ○ **A.** decorated
- ○ **B.** sparse
- ○ **C.** filled
- ○ **D.** overrun

5. <u>relish</u> the food
- ○ **A.** love
- ○ **B.** hate
- ○ **C.** swallow
- ○ **D.** spit out

6. <u>wary</u> movement
- ○ **A.** carefree
- ○ **B.** cautious
- ○ **C.** timid
- ○ **D.** quick

7. <u>inferior</u> brand
- ○ **A.** exterior
- ○ **B.** popular
- ○ **C.** superior
- ○ **D.** expensive

Reading Skills Practice Test 14

READING COMPREHENSION

Read each story. Then fill in the circle that best completes each sentence or answers each question.

SAMPLE

Americans love to roller-skate. Millions of people in the United States enjoy this fun sport. But did you know that roller-skating has been around for more than 200 years? It began in 1760. Belgian inventor Joseph Merlin was the first person to put on roller skates. Like many new skaters, he had trouble controlling them. After putting the skates on, he **inadvertently** rolled into an expensive mirror. Some things never change!

I. What is the best title for this story?
   ○ **A.** "Skating Mishaps"
   ○ **B.** "Merlin the Magician"
   ○ **C.** "Ice-Skating History"
   ○ **D.** "The First Roller Skater"

2. In this story, the word **inadvertently** means
   ○ **A.** purposefully.
   ○ **B.** accidentally.
   ○ **C.** quickly.
   ○ **D.** slowly.

A.   All dogs, from dachshunds to dalmatians, trace their family tree to one common ancestor—the gray wolf.

How did wolves become dogs? Humans chose wolves with certain traits—like size, shape, color, and gentleness—and then bred them with other wolves. For instance, small wolves that were bred with other small wolves would produce more small wolves. Over thousands of years, this kind of special breeding developed different kinds of dogs.

So, the next time some little pooch comes strolling down the sidewalk, give it a little respect. That doggie has some pretty tough ancestors!

I. Which of these would be the best title for this passage?
   ○ **A.** "How Wolves Became Dogs"
   ○ **B.** "All Kinds of Dogs"
   ○ **C.** "Wolf Behavior"
   ○ **D.** "Small Dogs Are Swell"

2. How did wolves become small dogs?
   ○ **A.** They mutated into dogs.
   ○ **B.** Humans bred them in certain ways.
   ○ **C.** They attacked the dogs and took their place.
   ○ **D.** They shrank from lack of food.

3. What is the purpose of this passage?
   ○ **A.** to inform you about how dogs share a common ancestor
   ○ **B.** to persuade you that dogs are great
   ○ **C.** to entertain you with small-dog stories
   ○ **D.** to scare you away from small dogs

B.   The sky is falling! Or so it seemed to a bunch of boys in Monahans, Texas. They were playing basketball one day when a meteorite, or space rock, landed just 10 feet from where they were shooting hoops.

The meteorite was a brown, 2-pound, 11-ounce, foot-shaped rock. The boys soon learned that it was a stony meteorite, also called a chondrite.

Meteorites formed billions of years ago. Usually, they burn up completely as they fall toward Earth and are called meteors. When a meteor doesn't burn up completely, it falls to Earth as a meteorite.

The mayor of Monahans thought the meteorite belonged to the town, not the boys. The boys disagreed. They wanted to sell the meteorite and use the money for college. The Monahans city council sided with the boys. The boys eventually sold the meteorite to a rock collector for $23,000.

I.   Which of these is a problem for the boys?
  ○ **A.** The mayor thought the meteorite belonged to the town.
  ○ **B.** The city council sided with the boys.
  ○ **C.** The boys sold the rock for $23,000.
  ○ **D.** Their basketball game got interrupted.

2.   What is the difference between a meteorite and a meteor?
  ○ **A.** Meteorites are meteors that do not burn up completely.
  ○ **B.** Meteorites are smaller meteors.
  ○ **C.** Meteors are small and meteorites are large.
  ○ **D.** Meteors are round and meteorites are foot-shaped.

3.   You can conclude from this story that
  ○ **A.** the boys are great basketball players.
  ○ **B.** meteorites are really common.
  ○ **C.** the mayor is an old man.
  ○ **D.** meteorites are valuable.

C.   In Atlanta, Georgia, hundreds of thousands of items are locked behind a steel door that isn't meant to be opened for 6,000 years.

The door fronts an airtight, watertight room that was once an indoor swimming pool. The room is filled with record albums, books, dolls, newspapers, watches, and recordings of old radio broadcasts.

Why fill a room with such treasures, then seal it for centuries? It's because the room is a time capsule. Its purpose is to send a message to the people of the future.

A time capsule is a container filled with objects that represent a particular part of life at a particular time. The Atlanta time capsule is called the Crypt of Civilization. It was sealed in 1940. Its creators chose items that would show all the achievements of human civilization, from the beginning of time through the 1930s.

I.   What is the main idea of this story?
  ○ **A.** Time capsules are easy to make.
  ○ **B.** People in the future will be very interested in us.
  ○ **C.** A time capsule in Atlanta is a message for the future.
  ○ **D.** Time capsules cannot be opened for at least 6,000 years.

2.   When was the Crypt of Civilization sealed?
  ○ **A.** 1930
  ○ **B.** 1940
  ○ **C.** 1950
  ○ **D.** 1960

3.   Why would people want to make a time capsule?
  ○ **A.** They want to get rich.
  ○ **B.** They want to keep special items safe from harm.
  ○ **C.** They want to become famous.
  ○ **D.** They want people in the future to know about us.

D.   Have you ever wondered where the words to our national anthem came from? The person to thank is a man named Francis Scott Key. He wrote them during the War of 1812.

Key had a good friend who was taken prisoner by the British during the War of 1812. Key was very worried about his friend. So he went to the British ship where his friend was being held prisoner.

The British agreed to let his friend go. There was just one catch. The British were about to attack Baltimore. The two men would have to wait on the ship during the attack.

It was a terrible battle. The British fired lots of bombs. The sky turned black with smoke. Key kept his eyes on an enormous American flag hanging over Baltimore's fort. As long as that flag was raised, American troops were surviving.

When the battle was over, the flag was still hanging! Key was so overcome, he pulled out an envelope and jotted down the words that would become our national anthem.

1. Why did Key go to the British ship?
- ○ **A.** He wanted to write a song.
- ○ **B.** He wanted to help his friend.
- ○ **C.** He wanted to watch the attack on Baltimore.
- ○ **D.** He wanted to escape the War of 1812.

2. Why did the sky turn black during the battle?
- ○ **A.** It was nighttime.
- ○ **B.** The British ship was on fire.
- ○ **C.** The American flag was on fire.
- ○ **D.** The British set off a lot of bombs.

3. After the battle, what effect did the sight of the American flag have on Key?
- ○ **A.** It caused him to cry for joy.
- ○ **B.** It caused him to write the words to our national anthem.
- ○ **C.** It caused him to hug his friend and the British soldiers.
- ○ **D.** It caused him to become angry and set off bombs.

E.   Bryan and Curtis were just sitting down at the computer when Javier came running in. He looked upset.

"I've lost my new scarf that my mom knitted for me! I can't believe it. I've looked everywhere. It's just gone. What am I going to do?"

"Calm down," Curtis said. "The best thing to do is to stop and think about where you might have left it."

"I already told you, I've looked everywhere," Javier cried.

"Are you sure? Maybe you forgot about some place you went. Tell us everything you've done this afternoon."

"Well, first I went by Coach Corran's office to ask about tomorrow's game. Then I rode my bike to the store to pick up some things for my mom. And then I came here to your house."

"Are you positive that's everywhere?"

"Yeah, I think so. Oh, wait a minute. After the store I stopped off at the deli to grab a snack. Oh, wow, I remember now. I left my scarf there!"

1. What did Javier do after he stopped by Coach Corran's office?
- ○ **A.** He went home.
- ○ **B.** He went to the store.
- ○ **C.** He went to the deli.
- ○ **D.** He went to Curtis's house.

2. What is the best title for this story?
- ○ **A.** "Fun on the Computer"
- ○ **B.** "A Valuable Scarf"
- ○ **C.** "Three Friends"
- ○ **D.** "Lost and Found"

3. Which of these adjectives best describes Javier?
- ○ **A.** bashful   ○ **C.** calm
- ○ **B.** forgetful   ○ **D.** fierce

4. You can guess that Curtis is _____
- ○ **A.** methodical.   ○ **C.** sarcastic.
- ○ **B.** unhelpful.   ○ **D.** bullying.

VOCABULARY
Which Word Is Missing?

In each of the following sentences, a word is missing. First, read each sentence. Then choose the missing word from the list beneath the sentence. Fill in the circle next to the word that is missing.

Sample:

As they waited for their big surprise, the children were _____ with excitement.
- ○ **A.** unhappy
- ○ **C.** breathless
- ○ **B.** bored
- ○ **D.** agonizing

1. Lisa's arms were bare, and she _____ in the cold.
- ○ **A.** trembled
- ○ **C.** sweated
- ○ **B.** screamed
- ○ **D.** argued

2. If Joey hadn't forgotten his house key, he wouldn't be in this _____.
- ○ **A.** adventure
- ○ **C.** excitement
- ○ **B.** voyage
- ○ **D.** predicament

3. The new action movie coming out next week is hotly _____.
- ○ **A.** criticized
- ○ **C.** unbelievable
- ○ **B.** anticipated
- ○ **D.** disgruntled

4. He was a good worker with an _____ job record.
- ○ **A.** extreme
- ○ **C.** atrocious
- ○ **B.** unblemished
- ○ **D.** outlandish

5. "I have to see your leader now!" he said with _____.
- ○ **A.** fervor
- ○ **C.** ennui
- ○ **B.** malice
- ○ **D.** tact

6. That was quite a _____ the scandal caused.
- ○ **A.** tirade
- ○ **C.** quest
- ○ **B.** triumph
- ○ **D.** sensation

7. The accused waited for the trial to start with some _____.
- ○ **A.** boredom
- ○ **C.** trepidation
- ○ **B.** glee
- ○ **D.** recreation

8. The thief _____ took all of her money and valuables.
- ○ **A.** genially
- ○ **C.** ruthlessly
- ○ **B.** gleefully
- ○ **D.** accidentally

9. She couldn't believe that the thief could be such a _____.
- ○ **A.** gentleman
- ○ **C.** personage
- ○ **B.** villain
- ○ **D.** savior

10. He's so _____, he would probably talk to an empty room.
- ○ **A.** reticent
- ○ **C.** fiendish
- ○ **B.** verbose
- ○ **D.** benevolent

11. I knew from her withering _____ that she was angry with me.
- ○ **A.** giggle
- ○ **C.** sob
- ○ **B.** glare
- ○ **D.** shrug

12. True chocolate lovers will not leave even a _____ of chocolate cake on their plates.
- ○ **A.** morsel
- ○ **C.** mortal
- ○ **B.** meager
- ○ **D.** variety

13. When airplanes were first _____, they were smaller and slower than today's planes.
- ○ **A.** improved
- ○ **C.** searched
- ○ **B.** repaired
- ○ **D.** invented

Reading Skills Practice Test 15

READING COMPREHENSION

Read each story. Then fill in the circle that best completes each sentence or answers each question.

SAMPLE

If you have a sweet tooth, you might have strong teeth. Researchers in Japan recently discovered that chocolate might help **prevent** cavities. They say the outer shell of the cocoa bean, the main ingredient in chocolate, fights tooth decay. One day soon, you could brush your teeth with chocolate toothpaste. However, until experts are sure, trading in toothpaste for a chocolate bar isn't such a sweet idea.

1. The best title for this story is
  ○ **A.** "Could Chocolate Prevent Cavities?"
  ○ **B.** "Sweets in Japan"
  ○ **C.** "New Ways to Brush Your Teeth"
  ○ **D.** "The Cocoa Bean"

2. In this story, the word **prevent** means
  ○ **A.** aerate.
  ○ **B.** stop.
  ○ **C.** deepen.
  ○ **D.** make.

A.   Did Martians once exist on our neighboring red planet? Researchers have discovered evidence that suggests lakes and oceans once covered Mars. And where there is water, there are often living things.

The Mars Global Surveyor, a spacecraft that mapped Mars, took pictures that show sedimentation, or layers of rock. These layers suggest lakes and oceans once existed on parts of Mars. If that's true, then Mars was probably a lot more like Earth in its early days than was **previously** thought.

Water and an atmosphere similar to Earth's would have given Mars the key ingredients for the creation of simple life forms. If life did once exist on Mars, there should be evidence in the form of fossils. To find the fossils, scientists will have to dig deep into the rock layers.

But even if there were Martians, they were probably tiny, and not the four-eyed green monsters you see in cartoons and comic books.

1. The main purpose of this article is to
  ○ **A.** convince the reader that people could never survive in outer space.
  ○ **B.** explain why scientists now believe life may have once existed on Mars.
  ○ **C.** discuss cartoon representations of aliens.
  ○ **D.** examine the difference between rocks on earth and rocks in Mars.

2. In this article, the word **previously** means
  ○ **A.** stupidly   ○ **C.** before
  ○ **B.** scientifically   ○ **D.** after

3. In order to find evidence of life on Mars, scientists will have to
  ○ **A.** dig deep into Mars's rock layers to look for fossils.
  ○ **B.** do research on the Internet
  ○ **C.** avoid looking at cartoons or comic books.
  ○ **D.** take new pictures with the Mars Global Surveyor.

B. Augustus Washington was one of the first African-American photographers. He was born in the early 1820s, when most black people in the U.S. were slaves, and he became a photographer when the art was new. Photography was first introduced in 1839.

Washington read books by abolitionists, people who worked to end slavery in the U.S., and developed a hatred of slavery. He **vowed** to become a teacher to help educate young African-American students.

He attended college, but quit when he could no longer afford the tuition. He became a photographer to earn money, and opened a studio in 1846 in Hartford, Connecticut. Abolitionist John Brown was one of Washington's most famous clients.

In 1853, Washington left the United States because the Fugitive Slave Act had been passed. It threatened his freedom, and the freedom all free black people in the U.S. Washington moved with his family to Liberia, a West African country founded by former slaves.

I. In this article, the word **vowed** means
○ **A.** grew. ○ **C.** refused.
○ **B.** promised. ○ **D.** traveled.

2. Which of these is an *opinion*?
○ **A.** Photography was first introduced in 1839.
○ **B.** Augustus Washington opened his photography studio in 1846.
○ **C.** The Fugitive Slave Act threatened Washington's freedom.
○ **D.** Washington must have been a smart, brave person.

3. You can infer from this article that
○ **A.** the weather in Liberia is always very hot.
○ **B.** Augustus Washington only took photographs of people.
○ **C.** Augustus Washington knew how to read.
○ **D.** John Brown was Augustus Washington's best friend.

C. Genetically altered food makes up more than half of the processed, or human-made, food consumed in the U.S. Coke, McDonald's hamburger buns, Heinz ketchup, and almost all bottled tomato sauces are just a few examples of food made with genetically altered soybeans and corn.

Genetically altered food, also called genetically **modified** food (GM food), is injected with bacteria and genes from other sources, like animals or nuts. Genes are parts of the cells of all living things.

Farmers plant genetically modified crops because the added genes work as pesticides, protecting plants from bugs that damage and kill. In theory, farmers can grow more crops and cause less harm to the environment.

But critics say GM foods need to be tested further by government agencies to see if they harm humans or the environment. Consumer advocates also believe that all foods which contain genetically altered materials should be labeled. That way, people can make their own decisions about what they want to eat.

I. In this article, the word **modified** means
○ **A.** changed. ○ **C.** disgusting.
○ **B.** delicious. ○ **D.** easy.

2. According to the article, farmers plant genetically modified crops because they
○ **A.** have a deal with McDonalds.
○ **B.** don't want to work hard.
○ **C.** are growing more of their crops in Washington, D.C.
○ **D.** want to grow more crops and cause less harm to nature.

3. From this article, you can conclude that
○ **A.** McDonald's stopped making buns with genetically modified ingredients.
○ **B.** some people wonder if genetically modified foods could hurt their health.
○ **C.** genetically modified foods taste better.
○ **D.** the government is taking more time to test GM foods.

D. Voting is the cornerstone of our democracy. Each U.S. citizen over 18 can vote. But this right did not come easily. Our nation's history is marked by the battles fought and victories won for voting rights.

Tens of thousands of Americans gave their lives fighting a long, brutal war against England from 1775 to 1781. The citizens of the newly formed United States did not want to be part of England, ruled by a king or queen. Instead, they wanted a democracy in which they could choose their own leaders who understood their needs.

After this war, African-American men still weren't **granted** the right to vote until the 15th Amendment was passed in 1870. Even then, some Southern states found ways to prevent African Americans from voting. These restrictions, called "Jim Crow" laws, were not outlawed until the Voting Rights Act of 1965.

Women also had to work hard to get the vote. Women did not win the right to vote until 1920, with the passage of the 19th Amendment.

1. According to this article, Americans fought to gain independence from England because
   ○ **A.** they didn't like the Jim Crow laws.
   ○ **B.** they didn't want a king or queen, but wanted to select their own leaders.
   ○ **C.** they wanted people to have to wait until they were 18 to vote.
   ○ **D.** they wanted women to be able to vote.

2. In this article, the word **granted** means
   ○ **A.** given.   ○ **C.** taken.
   ○ **B.** sold.   ○ **D.** denied.

3. In which year did women win the right to vote?
   ○ **A.** 1775   ○ **C.** 1920
   ○ **B.** 1870   ○ **D.** 1965

E. Baseball-card collecting may be all about David Wright or Albert Pujols nowadays, but baseball greats like Mickey Mantle and Willie Mays started the trading-card craze over 50 years ago.

A company called Topps began making the cards as a way to sell its Bazooka bubble gum. The gum isn't included anymore, but the cards are now an American tradition. Even George W. Bush traded the cards when he was a kid. He would send them to star players, asking for their autographs.

During the 1950s and '60s, children started tossing the cards into shoe boxes to save. Now some of those collections are worth thousands of dollars. The most wanted of the 2 $\frac{1}{2}$-by-3 $\frac{1}{2}$-inch trading cards are the "rookie cards," which are a player's first cards. Cards that are autographed are also popular. Old cards can be worth a lot, like a 1952 Mickey Mantle, which is valued at $18,000.

Baseball cards may have started out **linked** to bubble gum, but millions of cards later, the idea seems to have really stuck.

1. According to the article, Topps started making baseball cards because
   ○ **A.** people wanted to collect them.
   ○ **B.** George W. Bush liked baseball so much.
   ○ **C.** the company was trying to sell its Bazooka bubble gum.
   ○ **D.** they knew they would be worth a lot of money.

2. In this article, the word **linked** means
   ○ **A.** connected.
   ○ **B.** crazed.
   ○ **C.** chewed.
   ○ **D.** wrapped.

3. A good title for this article would be
   ○ **A.** "A Short History of Baseball Cards."
   ○ **B.** "How to Sell Your Baseball Cards."
   ○ **C.** "The Future of Baseball Cards."
   ○ **D.** "George W. Bush, Baseball Fan."

VOCABULARY

Synonyms

Read the underlined word in each phrase. Mark the word below it that has the same (or close to the same) meaning.

Sample:

extreme <u>fatigue</u>
- ○ **A.** tiredness
- ○ **B.** happiness
- ○ **C.** fatness
- ○ **D.** beauty

1. <u>arduous</u> task
   - ○ **A.** easy
   - ○ **B.** difficult
   - ○ **C.** lengthy
   - ○ **D.** daily

2. always <u>quarrelling</u>
   - ○ **A.** arguing
   - ○ **B.** moving
   - ○ **C.** talking
   - ○ **D.** singing

3. will you <u>surrender</u>
   - ○ **A.** come
   - ○ **B.** stay
   - ○ **C.** cry
   - ○ **D.** give up

4. use <u>caution</u>
   - ○ **A.** thinking
   - ○ **B.** carefulness
   - ○ **C.** protection
   - ○ **D.** help

5. <u>commend</u> his judgement
   - ○ **A.** criticize
   - ○ **B.** listen to
   - ○ **C.** praise
   - ○ **D.** accept

6. <u>appropriate</u> behavior
   - ○ **A.** mature
   - ○ **B.** immature
   - ○ **C.** proper
   - ○ **D.** wrong

7. <u>threatened</u> animals
   - ○ **A.** cute
   - ○ **B.** fierce
   - ○ **C.** in danger
   - ○ **D.** lost

Antonyms

Read the underlined word in each phrase. Mark the word below it that means the opposite or nearly the opposite.

Sample:

<u>esteemed</u> mayor
- ○ **A.** disrespected
- ○ **B.** respected
- ○ **C.** elected
- ○ **D.** elderly

1. <u>bonded</u> together
   - ○ **A.** joined
   - ○ **B.** living
   - ○ **C.** disconnected
   - ○ **D.** walking

2. <u>remote</u> area
   - ○ **A.** lovely
   - ○ **B.** grassy
   - ○ **C.** populated
   - ○ **D.** televised

3. <u>irrelevant</u> fact
   - ○ **A.** simple
   - ○ **B.** important
   - ○ **C.** forgotten
   - ○ **D.** agreeable

4. <u>meager</u> salary
   - ○ **A.** small
   - ○ **B.** big
   - ○ **C.** new
   - ○ **D.** professional

5. <u>exported</u> goods
   - ○ **A.** erupted
   - ○ **B.** fancy
   - ○ **C.** brought in
   - ○ **D.** sent

6. <u>unjustly</u> accused
   - ○ **A.** fairly
   - ○ **B.** sadly
   - ○ **C.** nearly
   - ○ **D.** personally

7. <u>stifle</u> a groan
   - ○ **A.** let out
   - ○ **B.** try
   - ○ **C.** keep in
   - ○ **D.** whine

Answer Key

TEST 1
Sample: 1.C 2.B

Passage A
1.A 2.B

Passage B
1.A 2.B 3.A

Passage C
1.D 2.B 3.B

Passage D
1.C 2.C 3.A

Passage E
1.C 2.D 3.B

Vocabulary
Synonyms
Sample: B
1.D 2.A 3.C 4.B
5.D 6.D 7.A
Antonyms
Sample: D
1.A 2.C 3.B 4.A
5.C 6.D 7.B

TEST 2
Sample: 1.B 2.C

Passage A
1.A 2.D 3.B

Passage B
1.B 2.D 3.A

Passage C
1.B 2.A 3.D

Passage D
1.D 2.C 3.D

Passage E
1.A 2.D 3. D

Vocabulary
Synonyms
Sample: A
1.A 2.D 3.A 4.B
5.C 6.B 7.C

Antonyms
Sample: C
1.B 2.A 3.D 4.A
5.B 6.C 7.A

TEST 3
Sample: 1.B 2.A

Passage A
1.D 2.D

Passage B
1.B 2.B 3.C

Passage C
1.C 2.A 3.B 4.D

Passage D
1.A 2.D 3.A

Passage E
1.C 2.B 3.A

Vocabulary
Synonyms
Sample: A
1.D 2.C 3.B 4.D
5.A 6.A 7.B
Antonyms
Sample: D
1.D 2.B 3.D 4.B
5.A 6.C 7.B

TEST 4
Sample: 1.B 2.D

Passage A
1.A 2.D

Passage B
1.C 2.C 3.C

Passage C
1.D 2.A 3.D

Passage D
1.B 2.A 3.A

Passage E
1.B 2.D 3.A

Vocabulary
Synonyms
Sample: A
1.B 2.A 3.B 4.A
5.B 6.D 7.D
Antonyms
Sample: D
1.C 2.C 3.C 4.C
5.B 6.D 7.A

TEST 5
Sample: 1.A 2.C

Passage A
1.A 2.C 3.C

Passage B
1.A 2.B 3.A

Passage C
1.C 2.D 3.A

Passage D
1.D 2.D 3.C

Passage E
1.B 2.A 3.D

Vocabulary
Synonyms
Sample: A
1.D 2.A 3.D 4.C
5.D 6.A 7.D
Multiple Meanings
Sample: B
1.B 2.C 3.B 4.C

TEST 6
Sample: 1.C 2.B

Passage A
1.C 2.A 3.D

Passage B
1.C 2.B

Passage C
1.B 2.C

Passage D
1.B 2.A 3.D

Passage E
1.D 2.A 3.D

Passage F
1.A 2.B 3.B 4.C

Study Skills
Reading a Bar Graph
1.C 2.A 3.B 4.D
**Reading a Table
of Contents**
1.B 2.C 3.B 4.D

TEST 7
Sample: 1.A 2.D

Passage A
1.A 2.B 3.D

Passage B
1.A 2.C 3.D

Passage C
1.D 2.D 3.A

Passage D
1.C 2.C 3.D 4.A

Passage E
1.A 2.A 3.C 4.B

Vocabulary
Which Word Is Missing?
Sample: C
1.B 2.C 3.A 4.B
5.D 6.B 7.C 8.A
9.A 10.C

TEST 8
Sample: 1.B 2.C

Passage A
1.A 2.B

Passage B
1.A 2.D 3.C

Passage C
1.A 2.A 3.C

Passage D
1.C 2.C 3.B 4.A

Passage E
1.A 2.B 3.D

Vocabulary
Synonyms
Sample: B
1.A 2.D 3.C 4.C
5.A 6.C 7.B
Antonyms
Sample: B
1.B 2.B 3.A 4.C
5.B 6.B 7.D

TEST 9
Sample: 1.A 2.B

Passage A
1.B 2.C

Passage B
1.D 2.D 3.C

Passage C
1.A 2.D 3.D

Passage D
1.B 2.A 3.C

Passage E
1.A 2.D 3.A

Vocabulary
Synonyms
Sample: D
1.D 2.A 3.C 4.D
5.B 6.C 7.B
Antonyms
Sample: A
1.B 2.D 3.C 4.D
5.C 6.D 7.A

TEST 10
Sample: 1.A 2.D

Passage A
1.B 2.C 3.A

Passage B
1.D 2.B 3.C

Passage C
1.D 2.A 3.A

Passage D
1.B 2.A 3.B

Passage E
1.A 2.C 3.A 4.C

Vocabulary
Synonyms
Sample: B
1.B 2.A 3.C 4.B
5.A 6.C 7.A
Antonyms
Sample: D
1.D 2.D 3.B 4.A
5.D 6.D 7.C

TEST 11
Sample: 1.B 2.A

Passage A
1.D 2.B 3.C

Passage B
1.D 2.A 3.C

Passage C
1.A 2.C 3.B

Passage D
1.C 2.A 3.B

Passage E
1.C 2.D 3.A 4.B

Vocabulary
Synonyms
Sample: B
1.A 2.B 3.B 4.B
5.A 6.A 7.B
Antonyms
Sample: A
1.D 2.A 3.A 4.A
5.A 6.C 7.B

TEST 12
Sample: 1.B 2.C

Passage A
1.D 2.A 3.B

Passage B
1.A 2.D 3.C

Passage C
1.A 2.C 3.B 4.A

Passage D
1.D 2.A 3.C 4.A

Passage E
1.D 2.D 3.C 4.B

Vocabulary
Synonyms
Sample: C
1.A 2.A 3.D 4.B
5.C 6.B 7.D
Antonyms
Sample: A
1.C 2.A 3.D 4.A
5.C 6.D 7.C

TEST 13
Sample: 1.B

Passage A
1.C 2.A

Passage B
1.C 2.C 3.B

Passage C
1.A 2.A

Passage D
1.B 2.B 3.A

Passage E
1.C 2.C 3.A

Vocabulary
Synonyms
Sample: B
1.A 2.C 3.C 4.A
5.B 6.A 7.B
Antonyms
Sample: C
1.A 2.C 3.A 4.B
5.B 6.A 7.C

TEST 14
Sample: 1.D 2.B

Passage A
1.A 2.B 3.A

Passage B
1.A 2.A 3.D

Passage C
1.C 2.B 3.D

Passage D
1.B 2.D 3.B

Passage E
1.B 2.D 3.B 4.A

Vocabulary
Which Word is Missing?
Sample: C
1.A 2.D 3.B 4.B 5.A
6.D 7.C 8.C 9.B
10.B 11.B 12.A 13.D

TEST 15
Sample: 1.A 2.B

Passage A
1.B 2.C 3.A

Passage B
1.B 2.D 3.C

Passage C
1.A 2.D 3.B

Passage D
1.B 2.A 3.C

Passage E
1.C 2.A 3.A

Vocabulary
Synonyms
Sample: A
1.B 2.A 3.D 4.B
5.C 6.C 7.C
Antonyms
Sample: A
1.C 2.C 3.B 4.B
5.C 6.A 7.A